"十二五"职业教育国家规划教材

经全国职业教育教材审定委员会审定

城市轨道交通客运服务英语

第3版

徐胜南 主　编

朱先威　李　真　副主编

梁晨溪 主　审

人民交通出版社

北　京

内容提要

本书为"十二五"职业教育国家规划教材。本书共15个教学单元，主要内容包括快速发展的中国地铁、地铁设备设施、地铁智能系统、日常问候、问路与指路、票务服务、地铁安检、地铁广播、失物招领、乘客投诉处理、大客流的应对、恶劣天气期间的作业、应急处置等。

本书结构完整、内容丰富，教学设计紧贴一线实际，着力培养学生的城市轨道交通客运服务英语口语对话能力，内容精炼、图文并茂，尽力为师生提供知识性、趣味性强的教学资料，激发学生的学习热情和兴趣。

本书可供职业院校城市轨道交通类专业及相关专业教学使用，亦可供相关行业岗位培训使用。

本书配套课件等助学助教资源，任课教师可通过加入职教轨道教学研讨群（QQ群：129327355）获取。

图书在版编目（CIP）数据

城市轨道交通客运服务英语/徐胜南主编.—3版.—北京:人民交通出版社股份有限公司，2025.1
　ISBN 978-7-114-19419-1

　Ⅰ.①城… Ⅱ.①徐… Ⅲ.①城市铁路—轨道交通—客运服务—英语—职业教育—教材 Ⅳ.①U293.5

中国国家版本馆CIP数据核字(2024)第036027号

"十二五"职业教育国家规划教材
Chengshi Guidao Jiaotong Keyun Fuwu Yingyu

书　　名：	城市轨道交通客运服务英语（第3版）
著 作 者：	徐胜南
责任编辑：	杨　思
责任校对：	赵媛媛
责任印制：	刘高彤
出版发行：	人民交通出版社
地　　址：	（100011）北京市朝阳区安定门外外馆斜街3号
网　　址：	http://www.ccpcl.com.cn
销售电话：	（010）85285911
总 经 销：	人民交通出版社发行部
经　　销：	各地新华书店
印　　刷：	中国电影出版社印刷厂
开　　本：	787×1092　1/16
印　　张：	9.5
字　　数：	300千
版　　次：	2015年7月　第1版 2020年12月　第2版 2025年1月　第3版
印　　次：	2025年1月　第3版　第1次印刷　总第13次印刷
书　　号：	ISBN 978-7-114-19419-1
定　　价：	45.00元

（有印刷、装订质量问题的图书，由本社负责调换）

第3版 前言

教材定位

"城市轨道交通客运服务英语"为城市轨道交通类专业基础课程。本教材从岗位工作需求出发，培养学生的专业英语能力，使学生在掌握城市轨道交通专业英语词汇和常用英语口语的基础上，更好地为来自世界各地的乘客提供服务和帮助。本教材也可作为城市轨道交通专业群中其他专业的拓展课教材。

编写理念

本教材为"十二五"职业教育国家规划教材，自2015年出版以来，选用广泛，在教学实践中反映良好，得到了普遍认可，有效提高了相关专业课程的教学水平和教育质量。

此次修订，由行业专家、学者及地铁公司专业人士全面参与编审，体现了"工学结合、校企合作"的理念。编写人员结合最新的岗位标准及专业教学内容，通过创设工作情境，全方位呈现城市轨道交通客运服务的全过程，有针对性地培养学生的英语服务表达能力，体现"以学生为中心""做中学，做中教"的职业教育理念。同时有机融入了职业精神、安全教育、传统文化、爱国情怀等课程思政内容，注重引导学生树立正确的世界观、人生观和价值观。

教材特点

1. 编写形式生动活泼

在充分开展企业调研和对职业院校学生学情进行分析的基础上，为了提升教材的实用性和可操作性，教材在编写形式上突破传统模式，学生可以通过教材中王东和莉莉等虚拟实习生的视角一起走进地铁，走向工作岗位，为乘客提供服务，再辅以讨论、角色扮演、拓展阅读等学习形式，提高学生的学习兴趣，达到教学目标。

2. 教材内容与时俱进

教材内容与城市轨道交通的发展趋势和专业课程标准紧密衔接，以企业真实的服务过程为导向进行编排，针对性强，重点培养学生的双语服务能力。历经多次修订，教材内容科学严谨，图文并茂，与信息技术有机融合，与时俱进，尤其是教材第3版在第2版的基础上，新增了Complementary Reading等模块，将新技术、新案例融入，提升学生科技素养、人文情怀、服务意识。

3. 教材内容编排宜教适学

教材内容符合职业院校学生的年龄和认知特点，循序渐进、宜教适学，适应职业岗位需求与学生可持续发展。从教学设计的角度，每个单元安排了Warm-up、Listening and Speaking、Reading and Writing、Self-Check等模块，通过图片、问题、情境设置等导入，激发学生学习兴趣，提高其分析、解决问题的能力；再结合小组讨论、角色扮演、交际活动、习题练习、趣味阅读等方式学习，既有利于提高学生学习的主动性，又有利于培养学生沟通表达的能力和团队合作精神。每个单元结束后，学生可通过实训及复习与思考进行自我考核，及时检查学习效果。

4. 教学资源丰富多样

为满足师生多样化、多层次的教学需求，同步开发了教案、多媒体课件、题库与知识树等信息化教学资源。

作者团队

参与本教材编写及修订工作的人员有：北京市自动化工程学校徐胜南，福建工业学校朱先威，北京市自动化工程学校李真、贾天丽、贺冬梅、姜婷婷、白云昕，北京交通运输职业学院李桃。徐胜南担任主编并负责全书统稿，朱先威、李真担任副主编，北京市地铁运营有限公司梁晨溪担任主审。

致谢

本教材在编写和修订过程中，使用教材的广大教师与行业专家提出了中肯的意见和建议，在此谨向他们表示感谢，同时感谢人民交通出版社为教材出版和资源配套工作所付出的努力。

最后，希望有关院校师生及读者对本教材多提宝贵意见，以便及时修订完善。

编　者
2024年3月

课程思政元素设计

本教材以习近平新时代中国特色社会主义思想为指导，设计和挖掘课程思政元素，培养和坚定学生的理想信念，提高学生的职业道德，讲好中国故事，把学生培养成为德才兼备、全面发展的高素质人才。

本教材以传承"讲仁爱、重民本、守诚信、崇正义、尚和合、求大同"的中华优秀传统文化为理念，以社会主义核心价值观"富强、民主、文明、和谐，自由、平等、公正、法治，爱国、敬业、诚信、友善"为要义，设计课程思政育人主题。围绕"知识传授、能力培养、素质提升"三维课程教学目标，以课程内容为载体，通过创设情境、听说读写、知识点梳理、融媒体等教学素材和方式的运用，用春雨润物细无声的方式向学生传递正确的价值追求和导向。在课堂教学中，教师可结合下表中的内容导引，结合相关的知识点或内容拓展，讲练结合，提升课程思政教学效果。

主题导引	思考与讨论	课程思政元素
Subway Culture	1. When did China's first subway operate? 2. Do you know the development of China's subway in recent years?	文化自信
The Fastest Subway	1. What speed can the fastest subway reach? 2. Where is the fastest subway located?	民族自豪感
CBTC	1. What is the CBTC? 2. What is the function of the CBTC?	科技意识 技术创新
Greeting and Introduction	1. How to greet your colleagues for the first time? 2. How to make an impressive introduction?	文明礼仪 友善 自信 沟通能力

主题导引	思考与讨论	课程思政元素
Ticket Service	1. How to sell a ticket in the Ticket Office? 2. What should the ticket seller pay attention to?	职业规范 爱岗敬业
Security Checks	1. Do passengers have to accept the security checks when they are ready to enter the subway? 2. What's the security checks for?	法律意识 认真负责 安全第一
Handle Lost Items	How to handle lost items?	诚实守信 严谨细致
Handle Complaints	1. What kind of complaints are there in the subway? 2. How to handle complaints?	责任意识 沟通与表达能力 解决问题的能力
Cope with High Passenger Flows	1. What is the high passenger flow? 2. How to cope with high passenger flows?	职业道德 沟通协调的能力 与人合作的能力
Deal with Extreme Weather	How to implement the duty in case of extreme weather?	吃苦耐劳 环保意识
Cope with Emergencies	How to cope with emergencies?	职业道德 安全意识 法律意识 与人合作
Passenger First Aid	What will you do if the passenger is in a serious condition in the subway?	敬畏生命 以人为本 乐于助人 科学意识
Good Service	How to offer passengers good service?	职业道德 服务意识

目录

Lead-in		1
Chapter 1	The Rapid Development of China's Subway System	3
Chapter 2	Subway Facilities and Equipment	13
Chapter 3	Intelligent Systems of Subway	23
Chapter 4	Greeting and Introduction	33
Chapter 5	Guide the Way	41
Chapter 6	Ticket Service	49
Chapter 7	Security Checks	57
Chapter 8	Subway Broadcasting	67
Chapter 9	Handle Lost Items	77
Chapter 10	Handle Complaints	85
Chapter 11	Cope with High Passenger Flows	95
Chapter 12	Deal with Extreme Weather	105

Chapter 13	Cope with Emergencies	113
Chapter 14	Passenger First Aid	121
Chapter 15	Have a Good Journey	131
References		140
附录1	候车、指路、安全乘车、出站、帮助等常见词汇与服务用语	141
附录2	宣传用语	142
附录3	文明用语	143
附录4	劝阻用语	144

Lead-in

With the rapid development of urban rail transit in China, specialized and high quality talents in the field of subway are welcome and have broad prospects. Lily and Wang Dong, who are majoring in urban rail transit operation and management, have just graduated from vocational school. Next, they will carry out an internship at the subway station. They are both determined to become excellent employees. The following are their main responsibilities.

Job Responsibilities

- Ticket Service
- Familiar with Facilities and Equipment
- Security Checks
- Subway Broadcasting
- Passenger First Aid
- Cope with Emergencies
- Handle Complaints

城市轨道交通客运服务英语
（第3版）

Chapter 1
The Rapid Development of China's Subway System

Objectives

1. Knowledge: Understand the characteristics of China's subways.
2. Ability: Talk about the development of China's subway system.
3. Morality: Be proud of the technical capabilities of China's subway system.

Suggested Class Hours

4 class hours

Warm-up

Guess which city's subways in the picture below.

| Beijing | Paris | London |
| Sevilla | Moscow | Berlin |

1. _____

2. _____

3. _____

4. _____

5. _____   6. _____

Listening and Speaking

Scene: Lily is very interested in the subway. Now, she is talking about the subway with her father who works at the subway station.

Dialogue A   Do You Know When China's First Subway Was Operated?

Activity 1: Listen and guess.

1. When did China's first subway operate?

_____

2. Which word has the same meaning with the word "metro"?

_____

Lily: Dad, do you know when China's first subway started operating?

Dad: Of course, I know. That's the Beijing subway, which started operating in 1971.

Lily: Why is the subway in Beijing called Beijing Subway, while the subway in Shanghai is called Shanghai Metro?

Dad: They both mean the same thing. Most subways in China are called METRO, and only a few cities are called SUBWAY.

Lily: I understand.

Dad: As we all know, China's subways have developed rapidly in recent years.

Lily: It is said that the Beijing subway ranks first in terms of safety and reliability in China and even globally.

Dad: Yes, you need to work hard and contribute to the development of China's subway system.

Lily: Okay, I will definitely work hard.

Activity 2: Listen again and try to fill in the blanks.

1. Most subways in China are called _____.

2. China's subways have _____ rapidly in recent years.

Activity 3: Work in pairs.

Practice the dialogue with your partner.

Activity 4: Role play.

Dialogue with given words.

Words and Phrases You May Use

subway   metro   contribute   develop   operate   rapidly

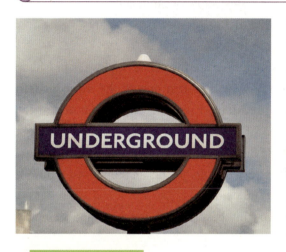

Words and Phrases

rapidly	[ˈræpɪdli]	adv.	迅速地	operate	[ˈɒpəreɪt]	vt.	运营
metro	[ˈmetrəʊ]	n.	地铁	subway	[ˈsʌbweɪ]	n.	地铁（美）
develop	[dɪˈveləp]	vt.	发展	contribute	[kənˈtrɪbjuːt]	vt.	贡献

Scene: Wang Dong is learning more about the world subway from his teacher.

Dialogue B   What Speed Can the Fastest Subway Reach?

Activity 5: Think and answer.

1. What speed can the fastest subway reach?

   _____

2. Is the train on the Daxing Airport Express unmanned?

   _____

Wang Dong: Can you tell me what speed the fastest subway can reach?

Teacher: The fastest subway can reach a speed of 160 kilometers per hour.

Wang Dong: Where are they?

Teacher: The fastest subway is in China. So far, there are four fastest subways in China. One is the Daxing Airport Express, which is also one of the most modern subways in the world. The Chengdu Metro Line 19, which operated at the end of 2023, also reached a speed of 160 kilometers per hour. In addition, Guangzhou Metro Line 18 and Line 22 also can reach that speed.

Wang Dong: The Daxing Airport Express is very famous. Is this an unmanned train?

Teacher: Yes. The Daxing Airport Express is unmanned.

Wang Dong: I will work hard to study and try my best to work for the China's subway in the future.

Teacher: Of course, you will, good child.

Activity 6: Listen again and try to fill in the blanks.

1. The fastest subway can reach a speed of _____ kilometers per hour.

2. The fastest subway is in _____.

Activity 7: Work in pairs.

Practice the dialogue with your partner.

Activity 8: Role play.

Dialogue with given words.

Words and Phrases You May Use

try one's best   modern   in the future   unmanned

Words and Phrases

airport	[ˈeəpɔːt]	n.	机场	Daxing Airport Express		大兴机场线
modern	[ˈmɒd(ə)n]	adj.	先进的	kilometer	[kɪˈlɒmɪtə(r)] n.	公里
unmanned	[ˌʌnˈmænd]	adj.	无人驾驶的			

Knowledge Expansion

1. The subway is an economical and efficient means of transportation.
   地铁是一种经济、快捷的交通工具。
2. The Beijing subway embodies traditional Chinese culture everywhere.
   北京地铁里处处体现着中国的传统文化。
3. China has the most subway lines in the world.
   中国拥有世界上最多的地铁线路。
4. The subways in China have experienced rapid development in recent years.
   中国的地铁在近些年经历了快速发展。
5. China's subway system is very advanced and efficient.
   中国的地铁系统非常先进且高效。
6. There are many beautiful and unique subway stations in China.
   中国有许多漂亮且独特的地铁站。
7. In China, subway has become an important means of transportation in people's daily lives.
   在中国，地铁已成为人们日常生活的重要交通方式。
8. China's subways carry a large number of passengers every day.
   中国地铁每天运送大量的乘客。
9. The safety and comfort of China's subways are widely praised.
   中国地铁的安全性和舒适性受到广泛赞誉。
10. Safety is always the top priority for subway operation.
    安全始终是地铁运营的首要任务。

Exercise 1

Choose Proper Words to Fill in the Blanks

1. That's the Beijing subway, which started _____ in 1971. (operating/operation)
2. The Daxing Airport Express is _____. (manned/unmanned)
3. The fastest subway can reach a speed of 160 kilometers _____ hour. (per/every)
4. I will work hard to study and try my _____ to work for China's subway in the future. (help/best)
5. China's subways have _____ rapidly in recent years. (developing/developed)
6. It's said that the Beijing subway ranks first in terms of safety and _____(reliability/reliable) in China and even globally.
7. Safety is always the top_____ for subway operation. (priority/choose)
8. China's subways _____ a large number of passengers every day.(ride/carry)
9. China has the most subway_____ in the world.(lines/line)

Exercise 2

Translate the Following Sentences into English

1. 未来我会努力学习，尽我最大的努力为中国的地铁工作。
2. 中国地铁近年来发展迅速。
3. 据说中国地铁是全球安全性和可靠度排名第一的地铁。
4. 安全始终是地铁运营的首要任务。
5. 中国地铁每天运送大量的乘客。
6. 在中国，地铁已成为人们日常生活的重要交通方式。
7. 大兴机场快线是无人驾驶。
8. 中国的地铁系统非常先进且高效。
9. 北京地铁里处处体现着中国的传统文化。
10. 中国拥有世界上最多的地铁线路。

Reading and Writing

The Chengdu Metro Line 19

The Chengdu Metro Line 19, which was fully operational on November 28, 2023, has become a new benchmark for urban subways in China due to its longest single line mileage!

The vehicle of Line 19 is a A-type vehicle, which with a maximum operating speed of 160 kilometers per hour. From design, research and development, manufacturing to assembly, it is entirely completed by Chengdu Rail Group and demonstrates the strong strength of China's rail transit industry.

The subway vehicles of Line 19 have adopted a series of advanced technologies, such as carbon fiber composite material body (碳纤维复合材料车体), new energy-saving and environment-friendly air conditioning (新型节能环保空调), etc., which have achieved significant results in lightweight, energy-saving and consumption reduction.

Words and Phrases

benchmark	['bentʃmɑːk]	n.	基准	carbon	['kɑːbən]	n.	碳纤维
maximum	['mæksɪməm]	adj.	极大/多的；最大极限的	assembly	[ə'sembli]	n.	装配
significant	[sɪg'nɪfɪkənt]	adj.	显著的				

Activity 9: Read and answer.

1. Which subway is the longest single line mileage in China?
   _____
2. What advanced technologies have the subway vehicles of Line 19 adopted?
   _____

Activity 10: Read and write (Read the following paragraphs and fill in the blanks with proper words).

| important | speed | earliest | operation |
| level | underground | run | system |

The Convenient and Efficient Subway

In modern cities, subway has become a kind of _____ means of public transport, which has high transport ability, fast _____, and is on schedule (时刻表). It also has independent (独立的) operation lines, without intersections (交叉) with bus or train routes. Besides operating in the underground, some subways also _____ above the ground.

The _____ subway system, the London _____, first opened as an "underground railway" in 1863, and its first electrified (电气化的) underground line opened in 1890, making the London Underground the world's first metro _____.

The first line of Beijing subway operated in 1971. Before the Beijing 2008 Olympic Games, there were three subways put into _____ in one year. The newly built subway equipment can reach the world-class _____.

Communicative Activity

Discuss the following topic in groups of five.
The advantages and disadvantages of subways.

Self-Check

I can speak and write:

☐ metro ☐ subway ☐ develop ☐ contribute
☐ passenger ☐ demonstrate ☐ airport ☐ modern
☐ efficient

I can translate these sentences into Chinese:

☐ 1.The Daxing Airport Express is unmanned.
☐ 2.I will work hard to study and try my best to work for China's subway in the future.
☐ 3.Can you tell me what speed the fastest subway can reach?
☐ 4.China's subways have developed rapidly in recent years.
☐ 5.The fastest subway can reach a speed of 160 kilometers per hour.
☐ 6.It's said that the Beijing subway ranks first in terms of safety and reliability in China and even globally.
☐ 7.China's subways carry a large number of passengers every day.
☐ 8.China has the most subway lines in the world.

Complementary Reading

How Many Names Do Subways Have in English?

The world's first subway was built in London, England in 1863, called Metropolitan and District Railway. At that time, they called the subway "the underground". Underground means "underground, hidden, secret", referring to railways built underground. But due to the length of this word, people tended to use it in spoken language, meaning "tube/tub". Because the subway looked like a big pipe at the time.

In French speaking countries, the subway is usually called "metro" in colloquial language, which comes from French Metropolitan. In its complete form, it is the metropolitan railway, which literally means "the railway in the city", or translated as "metropolitan railway". Later abbreviated as metro, it was absorbed by English and written as metro. Relatively speaking, metro is more universal worldwide. Most big cities use metro systems.

Subway is more commonly used in the United States. This word did not originally mean subway, but referring to "pedestrian underpasses". Sub means "below...".Subway originally refered to an underground passage that allowed people to walk through a busy road, was equivalent to the more familiar underpass. In 1897, the first subway in the United States was opened. In order to distinguish from the UK, the subway was not specifically referred to as underground, but the term "subway" was used instead.

Overall, the United States uses subway; Underground is used in the UK; In French speaking countries and most other regions, metro is used.

城市轨道交通客运服务英语
（第3版）

Chapter 2 Subway Facilities and Equipment

Objectives

1. Knowledge: Master the vocabularies of subway facilities and equipment.
2. Ability: Can explain the functions of subway facilities.
3. Morality: Become a subway staff with professional technical skills.

Suggested Class Hours

6 class hours

Warm-up

Today is Lily's first day working at the subway station. The following signs are the subway signs of some major cities in China. Can you guess which cities they are?

Beijing Subway   Dalian Metro   Chongqing Rail Transit   Chengdu Metro
Guangzhou Metro   Guangfo Metro   Hangzhou Metro   Harbin Metro
Hong Kong Mass Transit Railway (MTR)   Shanghai Metro

Listening and Speaking

Scene: Wang Dong is in intern in the subway company. He is discussing subway trains with Lily.

Dialogue A How Much Do You Know About the Subway?

Activity 1: Listen and guess.
1. What facilities are there in subway trains?
_____
2. What's the function of an Automatic Gate Machine?
_____

Wang Dong: What facilities are there in subway trains?
Lily: In addition to seats and handrails, there are also many visible facilities and equipment in a subway carriage, such as emergency communication devices, emergency unlocking devices, fire extinguishers, wheelchair stabilizers, etc. We all need to understand their locations and correct usage methods.

Wang Dong: What facilities are there in subway stations?
Lily: The facilities in subway stations mainly consist of these parts: escalators and elevators; Automatic Gate Machine(AGM); Platform Screen Door(PSD); Ticket Vending Machine (TVM) and station signs and broadcasting.

Wang Dong: Can you tell me how to use the Automatic Gate Machine ?
Lily: When using the Automatic Gate Machine, please stand outside the yellow line, hold the boarding card/code in the sensing area, wait for the gate to open, and pass quickly after it opens.

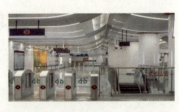

Activity 2: Listen again and try to fill in the blanks.
1. There are _____ in a subway carriage.
2. The facilities in subway stations mainly consist of these parts:_____.

Activity 3: Work in pairs.
Practice the dialogue with your partner.

Activity 4: Role play.
Dialogue with given words.

Words and Phrases You May Use

subway   seat   handrail   sign   Ticket Vending Machine   facility   equipment

Words and Phrases

handrail	['hændreɪl]	n.	扶手	seat	[siːt]	n.	座位
equipment	[ɪ'kwɪpmənt]	n.	设备	sign	[saɪn]	n.	指示牌
Ticket Vending Machine (TVM)			自动售票机	elevator	['elɪveɪtə(r)]	n.	电梯；升降机
Automatic Gate Machine (AGM)			闸机	Platform Screen Door (PSD)			屏蔽门

Scene: Zhang Qiang is Wang Dong's high school classmate. Now, he is discussing subway facilities with Wang Dong.

Dialogue B   What Are the Precautions for Using Subway Facilities?

Activity 5: Think and answer.

1. How to enter and exit the subway station?

_____

2. Can you say what the station signs and broadcasting are for?

_____

Zhang Qiang: Good morning!

Wang Dong: Good morning!

Zhang Qiang: Could you tell me how to enter and exit the subway station?

Wang Dong: When entering and exiting the subway station, we will choose to use escalators, elevators, or stairs. When using an escalator, it is necessary to hold the handrail tightly, do not lean, stand firmly with your feet. Do not step on the yellow line, Do not play on the escalator, and pay attention to the gaps under your feet. For passengers carrying large luggage, strollers or wheelchairs, it is recommended to use an elevator.

Zhang Qiang: Can you tell me what the station signs and broadcasting are for?

Wang Dong: In the subway station, it is recommended to carefully browse the relevant signs and travel information, while paying attention to the station broadcast and following the safety tips of the staff. When taking the train, you should follow the instructions and wait in the waiting area. After the train arrives, please get off first and then get on. Do not rush through the door.

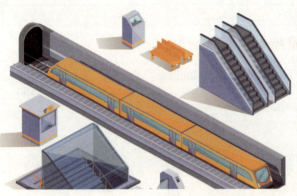

Activity 6: Listen again and try to fill in the blanks.

1. When entering and exiting the subway station, we will choose to use _____, _____, or stairs.
2. In the subway station, it is recommended to carefully browse the relevant _____ and travel information, while paying attention to the station _____ and following the safety tips of the staff.

Activity 7: Work in pairs.
Practice the dialogue with your partner.

Activity 8: Role play.
Dialogue with given words.

Words and Phrases You May Use

enter   exit   elevator   escalator   broadcast

Words and Phrases

exit	['eksɪt]	vt.	离开	
stair	[steə(r)]	n.	楼梯	
elevator	['elɪveɪtə(r)]	n.	升降电梯	
instruction	[ɪn'strʌkʃ(ə)n]	n.	用法说明	
escalator	['eskəleɪtə(r)]	n.	自动扶梯	
relevant	['reləvənt]	adj	有关的	
browse	[braʊz]	vt.	浏览	
stroller	['strəʊlə(r)]	n.	折叠式婴儿车	
wheelchair	['wiːltʃeə(r)]	n.	轮椅	

Knowledge Expansion

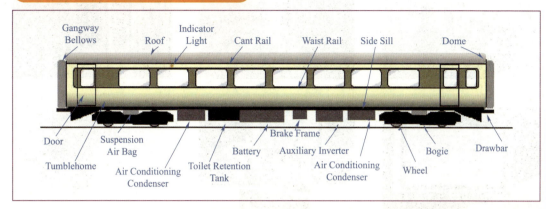

Gangway Bellows	通道折棚	Roof	车顶
Indicator Light	指示灯	Cant Rail	客车上侧梁
Waist Rail	腰梁	Side Sill	侧梁
Door	车门	Suspension Air Bag	悬挂气囊
Air Conditioning Condenser	空调冷凝器	Toilet	卫生间
Brake Frame	制动梁架	Wheel	车轮
Bogie	转向架	Drawbar	列车间的挂钩
Dome	车身穹顶	Tumblehome	车身内倾
Battery	蓄电池	Auxiliary Inverter	辅助逆变器
Retention Tank	储槽		

Exercise 1

Match the Following Pictures with the Given Words

1. Signs
2. Metro Vehicle
3. Automatic Gate Machine
4. Broadcasting System
5. Cab
6. PSL
7. Door
8. Information Screen
9. Security Inspection Machine

A (   )

B (   )

C (   )

D (   )   E (   )   F (   )

G (   )   H (   )   I (   )

Exercise 2

Translate the Following Words into English

闸机_____   自动售票机_____   信息提示一览表_____

屏蔽门_____   自动扶梯_____   垂直电梯_____

Reading and Writing

Track

  The track is the basis of railway operation. To give the train a good ride, the track alignment must be set within a millimeter. The track design and construction is a part of a complex engineering science involving earthwork, steelwork, timber, suspension system and the infrastructure of the railway.

The track is a fundamental part of the railway infrastructure, and also known as the permanent way. It consists of the rails, fasteners, sleepers and ballasts. The usual track form consists of the two steel rails, secured on the sleepers so as to keep the rails at the correct distance apart and capable of supporting the weight of trains. Traditionally, the sleepers are wooden. Nowadays, the concrete sleepers are more popular, and they are much heavier than the wooden ones, so they resist movement better. The typical concrete sleepers are as shown in the photos above.

Words and Phrases

track	[træk]	n.	轨道	alignment	[əˈlaɪnmənt]	n.	校正
be set			被设定	engineering science			工程学
suspension system			悬架系统	rail	[reɪl]	n.	铁轨
infrastructure	[ˈɪnfrəstrʌktʃə(r)]	n.	基础设施	sleeper	[ˈsliːpə(r)]	n.	轨枕
fastener	[ˈfɑːsnə(r)]	n.	扣件	concrete	[ˈkɒnkriːt]	n.	混凝土
ballast	[ˈbæləst]	n.	[交通](铁路)道砟				

Activity 9: Read and answer.

1. What are involved in the track design and construction?

_____

2. Can you talk about the track structure?

_____

3. Why are the concrete sleepers more popular nowadays?

_____

Activity 10: Read and write (Read the following paragraphs and fill in the blanks with proper words).

telephone　　fire equipment　　track　　equipped　　stations　　switch

Assistance Stations and Fire Equipment Cabinets

Every station platform is _____ with several assistance stations for emergency use. These cabinets include a direct _____ to the subway control center, a switch allowing the current to the _____ to be cut off, and a fire extinguisher. They are identified with the red or yellow hand signals, as well as special red or yellow lights in some _____. Several stations also have direct assistance telephones installed elsewhere in the station, such as in some far-flung accesses and automatic entries.

All station platforms are equipped with _____ cabinets at the end of the platforms. These contain a fire hose and a _____ allowing the power to the tracks to be cut off.

Communicative Activity

Discuss the following topic in group of five.

Wang Dong and Lily are introducing the names and usage methods of Beijing subway facilities and equipment to Zhang Qiang.

Self-Check

I can speak and write:

☐sign　　　　☐handrail　　　☐roof　　　　☐wheel
☐escalator　　☐toilet　　　　☐elevator　　☐broadcast
☐track　　　　☐suspension　　☐ballast　　　☐fastener
☐rail　　　　 ☐sleeper　　　 ☐concrete

I can translate these sentences into Chinese:

☐1.In addition to seats and handrails, there are also many visible facilities and equipment in a subway carriage.

☐2.What facilities are there in subway stations?

☐3.Can you tell me how to use the Automatic Gate Machine?

☐4.The track is the basis of railway operation.

☐5.Do not rush through the door.

☐6.For passengers carrying large luggage,strollers or wheelchairs,it is recommended to use an elevator.

☐7. Can you tell me what the station signs and broadcasting are for?
☐8. All station platforms are equipped with fire equipment cabinets at the end of the platforms.

I can:

☐ introduce the names and usage methods of subway facilities and equipment.
☐ generally introduce the tracks.

Complementary Reading

Universiade Themed Subway Station Unveiled in Chengdu

Featuring the 31st FISU (国际大学生体育联合会) World University Games, the subway station opened on Monday in Chengdu, host city of the biennial Summer University Games.

Rongbao, mascot (吉祥物) of the 31st FISU World University Games was on show at a Universiade themed subway station in Chengdu, southwest China's Sichuan Province, June 20th, 2023.

(Photo: China News Service/Liu Zhongjun)
(http://en.people.cn/n3/2023/0620/c90000-20034059-5.html)

城市轨道交通客运服务英语
（第3版）

Chapter 3
Intelligent Systems of Subway

Objectives

1. Knowledge: Master the vocabularies of subway supportive systems.
2. Ability: Can explain the functions of subway supportive systems.
3. Morality: Become a subway staff with professional technical skills.

Suggested Class Hours

6 class hours

Warm-up

Intelligent Systems of Subway

The subway adopts various automation equipment with electronic computer processing technologies as the core, replacing manual, mechanical, and electrical train organization, equipment operation, and safety assurance systems.

Please discuss the intelligent systems with your partner, and choose one you are familiar with from the options provided below to introduce their functions to your classmates.

FAS   ATC   SCADA   BAS   AFC

Listening and Speaking

Scene: Lily is visiting the subway station and discussing the PIS of the subway with the station manager, Mr. Zhang.

Dialogue A   Passenger Information System (PIS) of Subway

Activity 1: Listen and guess.

1. What's the function of PIS in the subway?
　_____

2. What are the three communication layers of PIS in the subway?
　_____

Lily: Good morning.

Mr.Zhang: Good morning.

Lily: Could you tell me something about the function of PIS in the subway?

Mr.Zhang: PIS of subway can provide passengers with all kinds of service information via Display Terminals in stations or train compartments.

Lily: What kinds of information can PIS provide us?

Mr.Zhang: It covers everything from passenger notices, timetables, automatic station announcements, weather forecasts, real-time news, live sports events, ads, and other real-time multimedia information.

Lily: Do you know the structure of this system?

Mr.Zhang: The PIS is divided into three communication layers, Central Control Unit, Sub Station Control Room as well as Display Terminals in stations and train compartments.

Lily: It's very interesting. Would you like to tell me more about these three layers?

Mr.Zhang: OK. The first layer, Central Control Unit, acts as the decision-making center and manages the whole system. The second layer, Substation Control

Room, can communicate with the vehicle-mounted control unit and pass the commands from Central Control Unit. The third layer, Display Terminals in stations and train compartments, can receive various kinds of information from Sub Station Control Room and display the information with LED information display screens.

Activity 2: Listen again and try to fill in the blanks.

1. PIS of subway can provide passengers with _____ in stations or train compartments.
2. The PIS is divided into three communication layers, _____ _____ as well as _____.
3. The third layer, Display Terminals in stations and train compartments, can _____ from Sub Station Control Room and _____ with LED information display screens.

Activity 3: Work in pairs.

Practice the dialogue with your partner.

Activity 4: Role play.

Dialogue with given words.

Words and Phrases You May Use

PIS   function   provide   display   terminal   Central Control Unit

Words and Phrases

Passenger Information System (PIS)		乘客信息系统	provide	[prə'vaɪd] vt.	提供
function	['fʌŋkʃ(ə)n]	n. 功能	Central Control Unit		中央控制装置
Display Terminal		显示终端	decision-making		决策
Sub Station Control Room		车站控制室	LED information display screen		LED信息显示屏
vehicle-mounted control unit		车载控制装置			

Chapter 3 Intelligent Systems of Subway

Scene: Zhang Qiang feels puzzled about the power supply system in the subway. Now, he is discussing this with Wang Dong.

Dialogue B　　Power Supply System of Subway

Activity 5: Think and answer.

1. How many components are there in the power supply system in the subway?

   _____

2. What is the third rail?

   _____

Zhang Qiang: Good morning.

Wang Dong: Good morning. What do you want to know about subway today?

Zhang Qiang: I feel so puzzled about the power supply system in the subway. Could you introduce it for me?

Wang Dong: Of course! It mainly consists of city electricity, Low-voltage (LV) distributors, UPS, computer controlled smart UPS and subsystems.

Zhang Qiang: I see. Are there two power supplies for the signaling system of subway?

Wang Dong: Yes, you are right. In addition, there are two modes of power supply for the subway: a third rail and overhead wires.

Zhang Qiang: What is the third rail?

Wang Dong: A third rail provides electric power through an additional rail (called "conductor rail") placed alongside or between the rails.

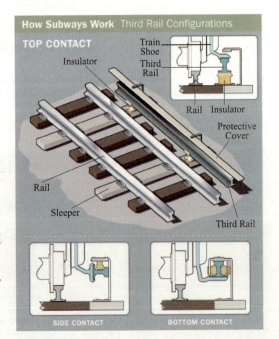

Zhang Qiang: I get it. Thank you.

Wang Dong: You are welcome.

Activity 6: Listen again and try to fill in the blanks.

1. It mainly consists of city electricity, _____, UPS, _____ and subsystems.

2. There are two modes of power supply for the subway: _____.

Activity 7: Work in pairs.

Practice the dialogue with your partner.

Activity 8: Role play.

Dialogue with given words.

Words and Phrases You May Use

puzzle　　third rail　　distributor　　power supply system　　UPS　　smart

Words and Phrases

puzzle	['pʌz(ə)l]	vt.	使……困惑	power supply system		供电系统
city electricity			市电	distributor	[dɪ'strɪbjətə(r)]	n. 配电盘
UPS (Uninterruptible Power Supply)			不间断电源	subsystem	[sʌb'sɪstəm]	n. 子系统
smart	[smɑːt]	adj.	智能的	third rail		第三轨
overhead wires			架空导线	conductor	[kən'dʌktə(r)]	n. 导体

Knowledge Expansion

1. BAS stands for Building Automatic System.
   BAS表示环境与设备监控系统。

2. BAS includes minor systems, major systems, water systems and tunnel ventilation systems and so on.
   环境与设备监控系统包括小系统、大系统、水系统和隧道通风系统等。

3. The minor system refers to the ventilation and air conditioning system in the station equipment room.
   小系统是指车站设备室的通风和空调系统。

4. The major system refers to the ventilation system in the public station area.
   大系统是指公共车站区域的通风系统。

5. In the BAS, sensors are installed at the supervision spot to measure physical data.
   在环境与设备监控系统中，传感器安装在监督现场，用于测量物理数据。

6. The functions of BAS include station environment monitoring, equipment management, system maintenance and so on.
   环境与设备监控系统的功能包括车站环境监测、设备管理、系统维护等。

7. UPS means Uninterruptible Power Supply. The function of UPS is to improve the reliabilities of subway power supply.
   UPS表示"不间断电源"。它的功能是提高地铁电力供应的可靠性。

Exercise 1

True or False

1. Power supply system only consists of city electricity, LV distributors, and computer

Chapter 3　Intelligent Systems of Subway

controlled smart UPS. ( )
2. There are two power supplies for the signaling system of subway. ( )
3. The function of UPS is to reduce the reliabilities of subway power supple. ( )
4. UPS means Uninterruptible Power Supply. ( )
5. The minor system refers to the ventilation in the station equipment room. ( )

Exercise 2

Translate the Following Diagrams of the Signaling System of a Subway Train into Chinese

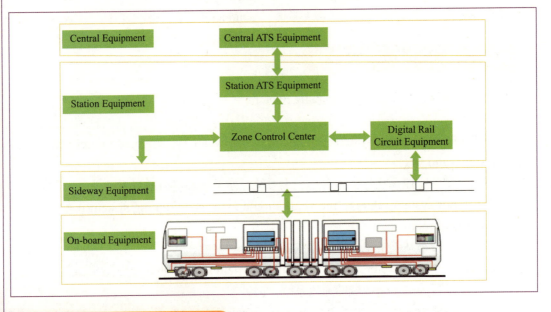

Reading and Writing

Fire Alarm System

FAS means Fire Alarm System, and it has at least three functions i.e. fire alarm, automatic spray & extinguishing, and alarm linkage. Basically it contains a supervising and managing center, IBP Emergency Control, detection device, alarm signal device, fire extinguisher, alarm sensor, control module and manual alarm. Automatic Fire Alarm System can be used to notify people to evacuate in case of fire, and to prepare the associated systems to control the spread of fire and smoke.

FAS can provide a dual management, comprising a main controller (control center) and subordinate controllers (stations). A hazard prevention monitoring center located in the control center is responsible for receiving warning signals and alarms, issuing disaster response commands, and monitoring the status of hazard prevention and resolution equipment along the entire line. In individual stations, hazard monitoring systems receive alarms and communicate in real-time with the command center, receiving and executing hazard-resolution commands.

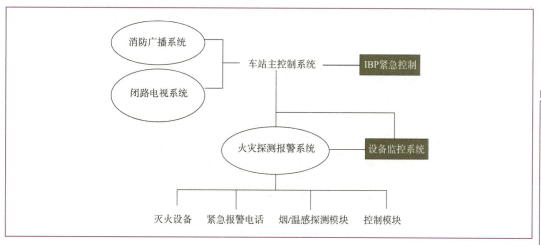

Words and Phrases

FAS (Fire Alarm System)			火灾自动报警系统	spray	[spreɪ]	n.	喷雾
extinguish	[ɪkˈstɪŋgwɪʃ]	vt.	熄灭	linkage	[ˈlɪŋkɪdʒ]	n.	联系
sensor	[ˈsensə(r)]	n.	传感器	alarm	[əˈlɑːm]	n.	警报
subordinate	[səˈbɔːdɪnət]	adj.	次要的	control module			控制模块
notify	[ˈnəʊtɪfaɪ]	vt.	通知	hazard	[ˈhæzəd]	n.	危险；危害

Activity 9: Read and answer.

1. What are the functions of FAS?
_____
2. What can FAS provide?
_____

Activity 10: Read and write (Read the following paragraphs and fill in the blanks with proper words).

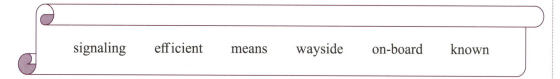

signaling   efficient   means   wayside   on-board   known

Brief Introduction of CBTC (基于通信的列车控制系统)

Nowadays Communication-Based Train Control (CBTC) is leading a new era (纪元) of rail transit (轨道交通) control. As a subway _____ system, CBTC makes use of telecommunication (通信) technology between the _____ (车载) equipment and the _____ (轨旁) equipment

29

to realize a safety distance between trains. The equipment is capable of implementing Automatic Train Protection (ATP), Automatic Train Operation (ATO) and Automatic Train Supervision (ATS) functions. By _____ of CBTC system, the exact position of a train is _____ more accurately (精确) than with the traditional signaling systems. This results in a more _____ and safer way to manage (管理) the subway traffic (交通).

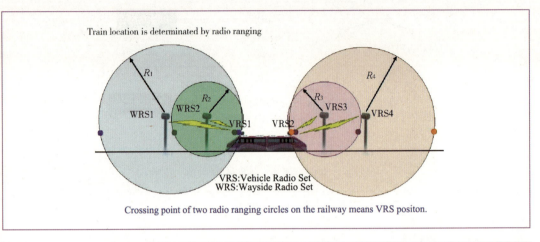

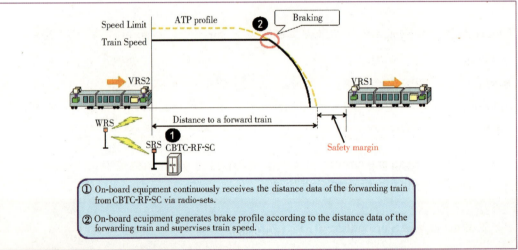

Communicative Activity

Discuss the following topics in groups of five.

Topic 1: As a member of the subway staff, do you know how many intelligent systems there are in the subway? Can you tell us what functions they have?

Topic 2: As a subway officer, you are supposed to obtain FAS certificate. Do you know anything about FAS certificate? Can you operate IBP?

Self-Check

I can speak and write:

☐ PIS   ☐ FAS   ☐ BAS   ☐ third rail
☐ alarm   ☐ UPS   ☐ smart   ☐ distributor
☐ power supply system   ☐ in case of   ☐ extinguish
☐ city electricity   ☐ Central Control Unit   ☐ LED information display screen

I can translate these sentences into Chinese:

☐ 1. PIS of subway can provide passengers with all kinds of service information via Display Terminals in stations or train compartments.
☐ 2. Are there two power supplies for the signaling system of subway?
☐ 3. The functions of BAS include station environment monitoring, equipment management, system maintenance and so on.
☐ 4. Would you like to tell me more about these three layers?
☐ 5. I feel so puzzled about the power supply system in the subway. Could you introduce it for me?
☐ 6. It mainly consists of city electricity, LV distributors, UPS, computer controlled smart UPS and subsystems.
☐ 7. FAS means Fire Alarm System, and it has at least three functions i.e. fire alarm, automatic spray & extinguishing, and alarm linkage.
☐ 8. There are two modes of power supply for the subway: a third rail and overhead wires.

I can:

☐ introduce the names and functions of the intelligent systems of the subway.
☐ generally introduce the functions of PIS.
☐ describe the working principles of FAS in the subway.

Complementary Reading

Air Conditioning System on a Subway Train

Modern subway trains are usually equipped with air conditioning system, which also has heaters. Here is the basic layout of an air conditioned coach, equipped with heating equipment.

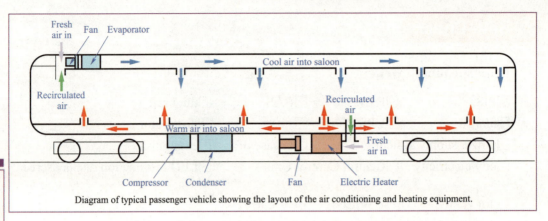

Diagram of typical passenger vehicle showing the layout of the air conditioning and heating equipment.

The air conditioning system is designed to the so-called "split" arrangement, where the condenser and compressor are mounted under the vehicle floor and the evaporator and fans are mounted in the roof. The coolant from the condenser is passed to the evaporator in the roof through a connecting pipe. The heater is a separate unit under the vehicle floor. Hot air is blown into the vehicle by the fans.

Do you think it is interesting?

Chapter 4
Greeting and Introduction

Objectives

1. Knowledge: Learn the vocabularies and sentences for greetings and introductions.
2. Ability: Be able to greet and introduce people.
3. Morality: Provide enthusiastic and thoughtful service.

Suggested Class Hours

4 class hours

Warm-up

Greetings and introductions are the basic manners of a subway staff. How to greet your colleagues and introduce yourself when you start working? Please practice this with your partner.

Listening and Speaking

Scene: Lily is visiting the Beijing subway before starting the internship. Zhang Hua and Xiao Liu received her.

Dialogue A   Welcome to Beijing Subway

Activity 1: Listen and guess.
Who is the station controller?

_____

Xiao Liu: Good morning. My name is Liu Wei. You can call me Xiao Liu. I'm a staff member of Beijing subway. Welcome to Beijing subway.

Lily: Good morning. I'm Lily. Nice to meet you.

Xiao Liu: Nice to meet you, too. Let me introduce my colleague Zhang Hua to you. He is a station controller.

Lily: Glad to meet you.

Zhang Hua: Glad to meet you, too.

Lily: Would you please tell me how many lines there are in Beijing subway?

Xiao Liu: There have been 27 lines by the end of 2023 in Beijing subway. It is very convenient to take the subway now in Beijing.

Lily: Yes, I think so. It's great.

Activity 2: Listen again and try to fill in the blanks.

It is very _____ to take the subway now in Beijing.

Activity 3: Work in pairs.

Practice the dialogue with your partner.

Activity 4: Role play.

Dialogue with given words.

Words and Phrases You May Use

welcome   glad   subway   station   colleague

Words and Phrases

colleague	['kɒliːg]	n.	同事	controller	[kən'trəʊlə(r)]	n.	管理者；控制者
convenient	[kən'viːniənt]	adj.	方便的	station controller			车站值班站长
introduce	[ˌɪntrə'djuːs]	vt.	介绍	glad	[glæd]	adj.	高兴的

Scene: On Wang Dong's first day working in the subway, Lily introduced him to her colleagues.

Dialogue B   I'm Very Happy to Meet You

Activity 5: Think and answer.

1. What does Xiao Bai do?

_____

2. What does Mr. Zhang do?

_____

Lily: Good morning, Xiao Bai. I'd like to introduce Wang Dong to you. He's our new colleague. Wang Dong, this is Xiao Bai, our station supervisor.

Xiao Bai: (Shaking hands with Wang Dong) Hello, it's a pleasure to meet you, Wang Dong.

Wang Dong: Thank you. I'm glad to meet you, too.
Lily: And this is Xiao Liu. He will work with you.
Wang Dong: Hi, Xiao Liu, I'm very happy to meet you.
Xiao Liu: Hello, Wang Dong, I'm glad to meet you. I've heard so much about you.
Lily: (Smiling) Only good things, Wang Dong. Oh, and here comes Mr. Zhang, the station manager.
Mr. Zhang: Hello, you must be Wang Dong. Pleased to meet you.
Wang Dong: Nice to meet you, Mr. Zhang. I'm looking forward to working with you.
Mr. Zhang: As far as I know, you are very suitable for this job. I'll arrange some work for you in the afternoon.
Wang Dong: Fine with me.
Lily: And this is Tang Hua. She's our security inspector.
Tang Hua: Hello, Wang Dong. It's good to see you.
Wang Dong: Hello, Tang Hua. Happy to meet you.

Activity 6: Listen again and try to fill in the blanks.

1. Hello, it's a pleasure to _____ you, Wang Dong.
2. As far as I know, you are very _____ for this job.

Activity 7: Work in pairs.

Practice the dialogue with your partner.

Activity 8: Role play.

Dialogue with given words.

Words and Phrases You May Use

meet　　happy　　suitable　　pleasure　　work

Words and Phrases

security inspector	安检员	look forward to			盼望
station manager	站长	suitable	['su:təb(ə)l]	adj.	合适的

Knowledge Expansion

1. Hello, how are you doing today?
   您好，今天怎么样？
2. Hey, what's going on?/Hey, how's it going?
   嗨，（最近）怎么样？
3. What's your major, please?
   请问你学的是什么专业？
4. Hey, what's up?
   您好吗？
5. Hello, It's my honor to meet you.
   您好，认识您是我的荣幸。
6. May I have your name, please?
   请问您如何称呼？
7. Hello, thank you very much for coming to my home/office/party/...
   您好，多谢光临寒舍/办公室/聚会……
8. Hello, I'm glad to meet you. I've heard so much about you.
   您好，很高兴见到您，久闻大名了。
9. Hello, it's nice/a pleasure/happy/good/pleased to meet you.
   您好，很高兴见到您。
10. Long time no see. How are you?
    好久未见了，您还好吗？

Exercise 1

Choose Proper Words to Fill in the Blanks

1. Oh, here _____ Mr. Zhang, the station manager. (come/comes)
2. Hey, what's _____ on? (going/ doing)
3. Hello, It's my _____ to meet you.(honor/honored)
4. I've _____ so much about you. (heard/hear)
5. I'd like to _____ Wang Dong to you. (introduce/introduction)
6. Hello, how are you _____ today? (doing/do)
7. Hello, Wang Dong. It's _____ to see you. (glad/good)
8. As far as I know, you are very _____ for this job. (suit/suitable)
9. Hey, how's it _____? (going/doing)
10. And _____ is Tang Hua. She's our security inspector. (this/it)

Exercise 2

Translate the Following Sentences into English

1. 您好，很高兴见到您。

2. 您好，见到您是我的荣幸。
3. 张站长走过来了。
4. 我非常期待能和您一起工作。
5. 您能告诉我北京地铁拥有多少条线路吗？
6. 据我所知，您非常适合这个职位。

Reading and Writing

Common Greetings

Common Morning and Evening Greetings

If you are greeting someone before noon, a common phrase is "Good morning". "Good afternoon" is also a greeting used after 12 p.m. If you're greeting someone in the evening or at night, it is usually to say "Good evening".

Common Slang Greetings

Some frequently used greeting slang phrases are "Hey, there" "What's up?" and "How's it going?" Words and phrases are also shortened by simply losing some of the words in the proper phrase. For example, "Morning" by itself is sometimes used in place of "Good morning". In the same sense, "Night" is also sometimes used in place of "Good night".

Common All Day Greetings

"Hello, how are you?" is a common greeting phrase. A simple "Hello" or "Hi" is also used commonly instead of the entire phrase. If you are just meeting someone for the first time, it is common to say "Hello, it is nice to meet you". If you haven't seen someone for a long time and are greeting him, it is common to say "Hello, how have you been?"

Words and Phrases

common	['kɒmən]	adj.	普通的；通俗的	frequently	['fri:kwəntli]	adv.	频繁地
entire	[ɪnˈtaɪə(r)]	adj.	全部的；整个的	proper	['prɒpə(r)]	adj.	适当的
slang	[slæŋ]	n.	俚语	in place of			替代
instead of			代替				

Activity 9: Read and answer.

1. If you are just meeting someone for the first time, how do you greet him?

_____

2. Which common greeting is used after 12 p.m.?

_____

3. What are common slang greetings?
_____

Activity 10: Read and write (Read the following paragraphs and fill in the blanks with proper words).

honor	have	major	though	help
along	realize	dreams	introduce	live

Self-introduction Speech

Good morning everyone, my name is Wang Dong. It is really a great _____ to have this opportunity (机会) to _____ myself.

I'm 20 years old and _____ in Beijing. I _____ just graduated (毕业) from a vocational (职业) school, and my _____ is urban rail transit operation and management. I love my major and study very hard. I also have a lot of interests, such as reading, singing and painting. _____ I tend to get nervous when making speeches, I get _____ well with friends and enjoy chatting with them. I am generally considered obliging (有责任心) and always willing to _____ others.

In summary (总之), I'm an ordinary boy with many dreams. One of my _____ is to be an excellent (优秀的) staff member of the subway. I have confidence (信心) to _____ my subway dream.

Thank you for listening. I am glad to have this chance to present myself to you. Thank you.

Communicative Activity

Discuss the following topics in groups of five.

Topic 1: To make a self-introduction to your partners. All of you will introduce the name, family background, educational background, hobbies and so on.

Topic 2: Xiao Zhang is a new colleague from the subway company where Wang Dong works. Wang Dong introduces Xiao Zhang to his colleagues and Xiao Zhang communicates with them.

Self-Check

I can speak and write:

☐ look forward to   ☐ station controller   ☐ enthusiastic   ☐ colleague
☐ station supervisor   ☐ station manager   ☐ convenient   ☐ frequently
☐ honor   ☐ common   ☐ slang   ☐ in place of

I can translate these sentences into Chinese:

☐ 1. Hello, it's nice to meet you.
☐ 2. Hello, how are you doing today?
☐ 3. What's your major, please?
☐ 4. May I have your name, please?
☐ 5. I've heard so much about you.
☐ 6. Hello, It's my honor to meet you.
☐ 7. Long time no see. How are you?
☐ 8. My major is urban rail transit operation and management.
☐ 9. Hello, how have you been?
☐ 10. What's up?

I can:

☐ greet people politely in English.
☐ make a proper self-introduction.

Complementary Reading

The "Wheel Deal" for Passengers at Shanghai Metro Station

Gao Yu deftly shuttling amidst large crowds on a self-balance scooter has become an iconic scene at Shanghai Metro's Hongqiao Railway Station, one of the busiest in the city's intricate metro network.

The 33-year-old director of the interchange station for metro Line 2, 10 and 17 has been serving passengers on her scooter for more than a decade, including almost every Spring Festival and holiday.

The practice has helped to improve the work efficiency of subway staffers by 30 percent and shorten the response time to passengers by half. The satisfaction rate among the passengers reaches 98 percent at the station.

Gao Yu serves metro passengers at Hongqiao Railway Metro Station.

(Source: SHINE Editor: Wang Yanlin)
(https://www.shine.cn/news/metro/2210031149/)

Chapter 5
Guide the Way

Objectives

1. Knowledge: Learn the vocabularies and sentences for guiding the way in the subway.
2. Ability: Can provide guidance and directions for passengers.
3. Morality: Provide passengers with patient and meticulous service.

Suggested Class Hours

4 class hours

Warm-up

Find the corresponding pictures from the following words.

| hospital | railway station | hotel |
| Tsinghua University | Tian'anmen | airport |

1._____

2._____

3._____

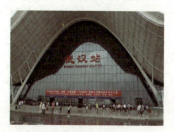
4._____

5._____

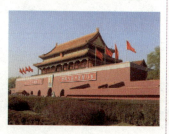
6._____

Listening and Speaking

Scene: Wang Dong is working at the platform and is guiding passengers on the way.

Dialogue A   Find a Restroom

Activity 1: Listen and guess.

1. Is there a restroom at the platform?

_____

2. What does the passenger ask?

_____

Passenger: Excuse me, is there a restroom nearby?
Wang Dong: Yes, of course. Take the escalator upstairs and turn right. Go straight ahead. There is one on the left at the end of the hall.
Passenger: OK, but may I ask where I can take the escalator?
Wang Dong: Yes, look ahead. Many people are taking the escalator on your right. Just go on and follow them.
Passenger: Thank you. By the way, is the restroom free?
Wang Dong: Yes, all the restrooms in Beijing subway are free.
Passenger: Thank you. I really appreciate it.
Wang Dong: It's my pleasure.

Activity 2: Listen again and try to fill in the blanks.

1. Where is the restroom?

_____

2. Is it free or not?

_____

Activity 3: Work in pairs.
Practice the dialogue with your partner.

Activity 4: Role play.
Dialogue with given words.

Words and Phrases You May Use

| restroom | upstair | free | straight | look ahead |

42

Words and Phrases

restroom	['restruːm]	n.	厕所；洗手间；休息室；更衣室	ahead	[ə'hed]	adv.	在（某人或某物的）前面
upstairs	[ʌp'steəz]	adv.	在楼上	appreciate	[ə'priːʃieɪt]	vt.	感激

Scene: Lily is working at the customer service center and is patiently answering the questions from the passenger.

Dialogue B   Where Should I Get Off?

Activity 5: Think and answer.

1. Where is the passenger going?

_____

2. What are they talking about?

_____

Passenger: Excuse me, can I go to the BJA Vocational School by subway?

Lily: Yes, you can take Line Changping to Zhuxinzhuang station first. Then transfer to Line 8 at the same platform across.

Passenger: Where should I get off?

Lily: You should get off at Lincui Qiao station, and exit from Exit C.

Passenger: Is the school right beside the station?

Lily: No, you still need to take a bus, and the bus stop is near the subway entrance.

Passenger: Which bus should I take?

Lily: You should take Bus No. 510 or No. 44. There's a stop at the school.

Passenger: Thank you very much.

Lily: My pleasure.

Activity 6: Listen again and try to find out the answers.

1. Does the passenger need to transfer?

_____

2. Where should the passenger get off?

_____

Activity 7: Work in pairs.

Practice the dialogue with your partner.

Activity 8: Role play.

Dialogue with given words.

Words and Phrases You May Use

platform	beside	exit
across	get off	stop

Words and Phrases

get off		下车	platform	['plætfɔːm]	n. 站台
vocational	[vəʊ'keɪʃən(n)l]	adj. 职业的	across	[ə'krɒs]	prep.; adv. 横过；在对面

Knowledge Expansion

1. The next train will arrive in three minutes.
   下一班车将在3分钟内到达。
2. How long will it take to get to Suzhou Qiao?
   到苏州桥需要多长时间？
3. Excuse me, could you tell me which line I should take to Fuxingmen?
   打扰一下，请问到复兴门坐几号线？
4. I wonder if there is a bank outside Line 5 Huixin Xijie Beikou.
   请问5号线惠新西街北口站出口附近有没有银行？
5. You can just take Line 10 and get off at Mudan Yuan station. The department store is right at the northwest exit.
   乘坐10号线，在牡丹园站下车，百货商店就在西北出口。
6. Excuse me, can I take Line 10 to Jishuitan Hospital?
   劳驾，乘坐10号线能到积水潭医院吗？
7. You can go straight ahead. Exit Ping'An Li station from Exit C and the bank is behind the station.
   一直往前走，从平安里C口出站，银行就在车站后面。
8. Go upstairs. The exit is at the east end of the platform.
   上楼，出口在站台的最东边。
9. Could you tell me how I can go to the subway station?
   请问怎么才能到地铁站？
10. Excuse me, can I go to the Summer Palace by subway?
    打扰一下，坐地铁能到颐和园吗？

Exercise 1

Choose Proper Words to Fill in the Blanks

1. Excuse me, is there a _____ nearby? (restroom/ATM)
2. Can I go to the BJA Vocational School _____ subway? (by/with)
3. How long will it _____ to get to Suzhou Qiao? (use/take)
4. Take the escalator upstairs and _____ right. (turn/choose)
5. There is one on the left _____ the end of the hall. (in/at)
6. Then transfer to Line 8 at the same platform _____. (across/cross)
7. Is the school right _____ the station? (beside/side)
8. You should get _____ at Lincui Qiao station, and exit from Exit C. (off/in)

Exercise 2

Translate the Following Sentences into English

1. 打扰一下，坐地铁能到颐和园吗？
2. 我应该坐哪路公交车？
3. 下一班车将在3分钟内到达。
4. 学校就在车站旁边吗？
5. 公交车站在地铁口附近。
6. 请问怎么才能到地铁站？
7. 上楼，出口在站台的最东边。
8. 请问5号线惠新西街北口站出口附近有没有银行？
9. 乘坐10号线，在牡丹园下车，百货商店就在西北出口。
10. 一直往前走，从平安里C口出站，银行就在车站后面。

Reading and Writing

Innovative Subway Wayfinding Services

The Xiaozhai Station of Xi'an Metro, a transfer station between Line 2 and Line 3, is encircled by numerous business districts and boasts the highest passenger traffic within the Xi'an Metro network. The staff report that countless individuals seek directions daily. To streamline this process, the VR guidance system at Xiaozhai Station has been launched.

The station master Liu at Xiaozhai Station of Xi'an Metro, remarked: "We have positioned a QR(Quick Response) code at the station's service desk, enabling passengers to access the VR(Virtual Reality) guidance system through a simple QR code scan." The VR guidance system offers a comprehensive overview of the station's layout, allowing users to quickly switch between different scenes with a single click. This visual interface enables passengers to swiftly understand the spatial arrangement, transfer connections, and exit details of the station.

To enhance the travel experience of the elderly passengers, Zhengzhou Metro Line 3 has introduced a heartwarming service—the "Little Orange" convenience route card. When you are riding Line 3 and need to transfer to another line but cannot remember where to transfer, you can come to the customer service center or platform area to seek assistance from the staff. The staff will fill out a "customized" route card for you based on your destination. The card contains detailed route and transfer information, with clear and large font, making it easy for elderly passengers to read. With the guidance of the route card, passengers can easily reach their destination, saving time and worries.

Innovative subway wayfinding services make travel more convenient and efficient. In the future, we look forward to more innovative services to bring passengers a better travel experience.

Words and Phrases

streamline	[ˈstriːmlaɪn]	v.	使……更加高效；使……流线化	interface	[ˈɪntəfeɪs]	n. 界面
launch	[lɔːntʃ]	v.	启动；发射	spatial	[ˈspeɪʃ(ə)l]	adj. 空间的
virtual	[ˈvɜːtʃuəl]	adj.	虚拟的	customized	[ˈkʌstəmaɪzd]	adj. 定制的；个性化的
comprehensive	[ˌkɒmprɪˈhensɪv]	adj.	全面的；综合的	innovative	[ˈɪnəveɪtɪv]	adj. 创新的
layout	[ˈleɪaʊt]	n.	布局			

Activity 9: Read and answer.

1. What is the purpose of the VR guidance system at Xiaozhai Station?

_____

2. What kind of innovative subway wayfinding service does Zhengzhou Metro offer to the elderly passengers?

_____

Activity 10: Read and write (Read the following paragraphs and fill in the blanks with proper words).

across	basic	direct	give	helpful	in mind
opposite	polite	straight	traffic	kind	

How to Give Directions

As a subway staff, you must be familiar with every station and surrounding areas near the subway lines. Also, you should know how to _____ the way. When you are asked like "How can I get to Wangfujing Street?" or "How can I get to the washroom?" It's OK to give _____ directions with short sentences like "Take Line 2 and get off right at the station. You can't miss it." Phrases like "The best way is to ..." "The quickest way is to ... " are also very useful.

When you _____ directions, remember to speak slowly and spell out the words if necessary. You should keep _____ some useful phrases and sentences. They are "Go _____ ahead." "Turn right till you see the _____ lights." "Go _____ the street. The subway station is just _____ to the post office." etc.

You can repeat your directions so that they can be understood better and more clearly. If you don't hear the questions clearly, you can say "I beg your pardon?" or just "Repeat, please."

Sometimes simple drawings of the directions are _____. Meantime, when you give directions, remember words like "Please" or "Excuse me,..." It is _____ and _____.

Chapter 5 Guide the Way

🌀 Communicative Activity

Discuss the following topics in groups of five.

Topic 1: Jack and his wife, Mary, both French, just arrived in Beijing for the first time. Now they are on the platform at Jishuitan Station, Line 2. They are going to the Summer Palace by subway. They are asking Wang Dong and Lily, who are the station attendants for directions. Wang Dong and Lily will help them patiently and efficiently.

Topic 2: Tina, a foreign student, just got off the train at Shahe Univ. Park Station. She wonders how she can go to the Central University of Finance and Economics. As a station attendant, you are going to guide Tina.

🌀 Self-Check

I can speak and write:

☐ restroom ☐ appreciate ☐ platform

☐ streamline   ☐ comprehensive   ☐ customized

I can translate these sentences into Chinese:

☐ 1. I wonder if there is a bank outside Line 5 Huixin Xijie Beikou.
☐ 2. Excuse me, can I take Line 10 to Jishuitan Hospital?
☐ 3. Go upstairs. The exit is at the east end of the platform.
☐ 4. Excuse me, can I go to the Summer Palace by subway?

I can:

☐ ask for and give directions in the subway in English.
☐ use proper expressions for guiding the way.

Complementary Reading

We're Here to Help You!

Welcome to the subway! If you're new to the city or simply need some guidance to find your way, don't worry, we're here to help you. Whether you're looking to explore the city's attractions or get to a specific destination, our subway system has got you covered.

To start, each subway station is equipped with clear signage, displaying the names of the lines and directions. Make sure to check the maps posted on the walls or use the digital displays for real-time train schedules.

When asking for directions or assistance, feel free to approach our friendly station staffs. They are easily identifiable by their uniforms and name tags. Don't hesitate to ask questions like "Could you please tell me which line I should take to reach [destination]?" or "Can you guide me to the nearest transfer station?"

Alternatively, rely on the help of fellow commuters. People in the subway are often willing to lend a hand and share their knowledge about the best routes. Polite phrases such as "Excuse me, can you tell me how many stops to [destination]?" or "Do you know if this train goes to [destination]?" can go a long way in initiating conversation and getting the information you need.

Additionally, our stations are equipped with detailed route maps and diagrams both inside the trains and at key points throughout the stations. Take a moment to familiarize yourself with the subway map, so you can navigate through the lines and understand the different transfer points.

Remember, it's essential to always be aware of your surroundings and follow the station rules for safety. Finally, we hope your subway journey is smooth and enjoyable, and feel free to ask for assistance whenever needed. Have a great trip!

Chapter 6
Ticket Service

🌾 Objectives

1. Knowledge: Learn the vocabularies and sentences of ticket sales in the subway customer service centers.
2. Ability: Be able to sell tickets in English.
3. Morality: Provide accurately and efficiently ticket services.

🌱 Suggested Class Hours

4 class hours

🌾 Warm-up

Wang Dong is a subway ticket seller. Look at the picture, what's he holding in his hand? What kind of information can you get from this picture?

🌾 Listening and Speaking

Scene: Wang Dong works at the subway ticket office, and some passengers are queuing up to buy tickets.

Dialogue A   How Many Tickets Do You Want?

Activity 1: Listen and guess.
1. How many tickets does the passenger want to buy?

_____

2. Does the passenger have enough change?

_____

49

Wang Dong: How many tickets do you want?
Passenger: Three tickets to Xidan, please. How much?
Wang Dong: That's nine yuan.
Passenger: Here's fifty yuan.
Wang Dong: Do you have any change? I can't find it.
Passenger: Sorry, I don't have enough change.
Wang Dong: Don't worry! Wait a minute, please. (A moment later…) Thank you for your patience. Here're your tickets and change.
Passenger: Thank you.
Wang Dong: You are welcome.

Activity 2: Listen again and try to fill in the blanks.
1. Do you have any _____? I can't _____ it.
2. Here're your _____ and change.

Activity 3: Work in pairs.
Practice the dialogue with your partner.

Activity 4: Role play.
Dialogue with given words.

Words and Phrases You May Use

ticket   office   change   welcome   how much

Words and Phrases

patience	['peɪʃ(ə)ns]	n.	耐心	ticket seller			售票员
ticket	['tɪkɪt]	n.	车票	passenger	['pæsɪndʒə(r)]	n.	乘客
change	[tʃeɪndʒ]	n.	零钱	enough	[ɪ'nʌf]	adj.	足够的
service	['sɜːvɪs]	n.	服务				

Scene: Lily is a ticket inspector who stands at the entrance to provide services for passengers to enter the subway station with their tickets.

Dialogue B   Please Check Your Ticket Here

Activity 5: Think and answer.
1. What problem does the passenger encounter?
_____
2. What advice does Lily give to the passenger?
_____

Lily: Don't worry, please queue up here to check your tickets.
Passenger: Hello! Staff, I can't swipe my subway ticket.

Lily: Try again please.

Passenger: I still can't swipe it. What should I do?

Lily: Could you please go to the ticket center to handle it?

Passenger: OK, thanks a lot!

Activity 6: Listen again and try to fill in the blanks.

1. Please _____ to check your tickets.

2. Could you please go to the ticket center to _____ it?

Activity 7: Work in pairs.

Practice the dialogue with your partner.

Activity 8: Role play.

Dialogue with given words.

Words and Phrases You May Use

check   ticket center   handle   queue up

Words and Phrases

queue up	排队			encounter	[ɪnˈkaʊntə(r)]	vt.	面对
check	[tʃek]	vt.	检查				

51

Knowledge Expansion

The Different Types of Subway Tickets

Here are the different types of subway tickets:

1. Single Ride Ticket: This ticket allows a passenger to travel from one station to another on a single trip. It is valid for one-time use only and is usually purchased at the station before getting on the subway.
2. Multiple Ride Ticket: Also known as a "multi-ride" or "bulk" ticket, this option allows passengers to purchase multiple rides in advance. These tickets often have a discounted price compared to single ride tickets.
3. Day Pass: A day pass is valid for unlimited travel within a specified period, usually a full day. With a day pass, passengers can hop on and off the subway as many times as they wish during the designated day.
4. Weekly/Monthly Pass: These passes are suitable for regular commuters. They offer unlimited travel for a specific duration, such as a week or a month. Commuters can save money by purchasing these passes instead of buying individual tickets every day.
5. Reduced Fare Pass: Many subway systems offer reduced fare passes for the senior citizens, students, people with disabilities, or other eligible groups. These passes typically require verification of eligibility and offer discounted rates for the designated users.
6. Tourist Pass: Some cities offer special tourist passes that allow visitors to explore the subway system without worrying about fares. These passes often include some additional benefits, such as free entry to museums or discounts at various attractions.

Exercise 1

Choose Proper Words to Fill in the Blanks

1. Do you have any _____ ? (change/changes)
2. Thank you for your _____ . (patient/patience)
3. Here're your _____ and change. (ticket/tickets)
4. Please _____ here to check your tickets. (line on/queue up)
5. I can't _____ my subway ticket. (swiped/swipe)
6. Could you please go to the ticket center to _____ it? (hand/handle)
7. Try _____ please. (again/across)
8. Wang Dong is a subway ticket _____ . (seller/sell)
9. Three tickets to Xidan, please. _____ ? (Hou much/How many)

Exercise 2

Translate the Following Sentences into English

1. 请再试一次。
2. 你有零钱吗？我找不开。
3. 这是您的车票和零钱。
4. 请问您需要购买几张车票？
5. 您能去票务中心处理一下吗？
6. 请等一下。
7. 不要拥挤，请排好队检票。
8. 我刷不了我的地铁票。
9. 感谢您的耐心。
10. 我的零钱不够。

Reading and Writing

How Can You Purchase Tickets with the TVM?

Here's how you can purchase tickets with the Ticket Vending Machine(TVM):

(1) Locate the TVMs: Look for TVMs located within the subway station. They are usually prominently placed near the entrances or in the ticketing area.

(2) Choose your language: Most TVMs have language options. Select your preferred language, which is often displayed on the screen.

(3) Select the ticket type: Once you've selected your language, the TVM will present you with various ticket options. These may include single ride tickets, day passes, weekly or monthly passes, etc. Choose the ticket type that suits your needs.

(4) Enter payment: The TVM will accept cash, coins, and sometimes credit/debit cards. Insert your payment method as instructed by the machine.

(5) Select the number of tickets: Depending on the ticket type you choose, you may be prompted to select the number of tickets you wish to purchase. Use the keypad or touch screen to input the desired quantity.

(6) Collect your ticket(s): After completing the payment and ticket selection process, the TVM will dispense your ticket(s). Be sure to collect your ticket(s) before proceeding.

(7) Validate the ticket (if required): Some subway systems require passengers to validate their tickets before getting on the subway. This is often done by inserting the ticket into a validation machine or tapping it on a card reader at the entrance gate.

Follow the instructions provided in the station. Remember to keep your ticket handy throughout your journey as you may be required to show it to the ticket inspectors or upon exiting the station. If you have any difficulties or questions, don't hesitate to ask the station staff for assistance.

Words and Phrases

payment	['peɪmənt]	n.	支付额	insert	[ɪn'sɜːt]	vt.	插入
credit	['kredɪt]	n.	信用	touch screen			触摸屏
debit	['debɪt]	n.	借记	keypad	['kiːpæd]	n.	按键

Activity 9: Read and answer.

1. What's the advantage of the TVM?
　_____
2. How to help a passenger buy a subway ticket through the TVM?
　_____
3. How to validate the ticket before getting on the subway if required?
　_____

Activity 10: Read and write (Read the following paragraphs and fill in the blanks with proper words).

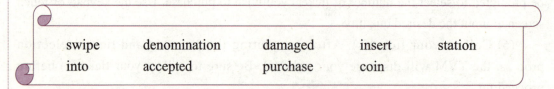

| swipe | denomination | damaged | insert | station |
| into | accepted | purchase | coin | |

Single Journey Ticket for Beijing Subway

　　When the AFC (Automatic Fare Collection) system goes _____ effect, only two kinds of tickets are _____ for transportation (交通) on the Beijing subway lines: the single journey tickets (单程票) and the YIKATONG that is already in use.

The AFC system allows commuters to _____ single journey tickets at TVMs, which only takes 1 yuan _____ or crisp 5 and 10 yuan notes. Those with banknotes of larger _____ must purchase tickets from actual ticket counters. The new single journey tickets are environment-friendly, as each ticket may be used to serve 2,500-3,000 trips, if they are not _____.

Those using the YIKATONG must _____ their tickets again when exiting the subway station. Customers using the single journey tickets must _____ their tickets into the Automatic Gate Machines at the exit. Only after the tickets are accepted by the machine can the travelers leave the _____.

Communicative Activity

Discuss the following topic in groups of five.

Peter is from Pakistan. He prefers to buy a single journey ticket. A station staff is telling him how to use the Ticket Vending Machine (TVM).

Self-Check

I can speak and write:

- ☐ ticket
- ☐ change
- ☐ valid
- ☐ touch screen
- ☐ service
- ☐ benefit
- ☐ exit
- ☐ ticket inspector
- ☐ coin
- ☐ check
- ☐ discount
- ☐ queue up
- ☐ suitable
- ☐ swipe
- ☐ prominently

I can translate these sentences into Chinese:

☐ 1. Try again please.
☐ 2. How many tickets do you want?

☐3.Here're your tickets and change.
☐4.Please queue up here to check your tickets.
☐5.I can't swipe my subway ticket.
☐6.Could you please go to the ticket center to handle it?
☐7.Do you have any change?
☐8.Thank you for your patience!
☐9.You are welcome.

I can:

☐handle ticket related issues.
☐guide passengers to purchase tickets.

Complementary Reading

Beijing Pilots Palm-Print Subway Ticket

BEIJING, May 21 (Xinhua) -No need to swipe a card or scan a QR code. A Beijing subway line now allows passengers to enter and exit "empty-handed" by scanning the palms of their hands.

A pilot program launched on Sunday to apply the new technology on the Daxing Airport Express, which links the Beijing Daxing International Airport, said the Beijing Municipal Commission of Transport.

Passengers can show their palms to pass ticket gates at stops along the line after inputting their palm information at the station's ticket machines and authorizing(授权) the use via WeChat, a popular messaging App in China. Fees are automatically deducted after exit.

The ticket gates recognize the user's palm print and veins without contact, said the commission. It can allow passengers to take subway trains if they do not have cash when their smartphones run out of battery.

The commission said data masking and encryption technologies have been applied to protect the users' information.

(Source: Xinhua 2023-05-21)
(https://english.news.cn/20230521/bd86cab15a1a481684dd21e28981b8aa/c.html)

Chapter 7
Security Checks

Objectives

1. Knowledge: Learn the vocabularies and sentences of subway security checks.
2. Ability: Be familiar with the procedures and steps of subway security checks.
3. Morality: Strong safety awareness.

Suggested Class Hours

4 class hours

Warm-up

Before entering the subway for a ride, you need to undergo a safety check. Look at the following pictures and talk to your classmates about your views on subway security checks.

Listening and Speaking

Scene: As a security inspector, Wang Dong is working when a person goes in while other passengers are being screened. Wang Dong stop him. Why does he refuse security checks? What will happen next?

Dialogue A What's the Security Check for?

Activity 1: Listen and guess.

1. Do passengers need to go through security check when entering the subway station?

_____

2. What's the security check for?

_____

Wang Dong: Good morning, sir. Security check, please.

Passenger: Security check? Oh, I just have some books in my bag.

Wang Dong: Everyone must undergo a security check, including their luggages, according subway regulations.

Passenger: OK. I'll follow the rules.

Wang Dong: Please put your bag on the conveyor belt and pass it through the X-ray machine.

Passenger: OK!

After passing the X-ray machine, the man is about to leave with his bag when Wang Dong stops him.

Wang Dong: Sir. Please wait, is there a bottle of water in your bag?

Passenger: Yes, what's wrong?

Wang Dong: Could you please open it and take a sip.

Passenger: Okey. (the man took a sip) I don't know why you're so strict. What's the security check for?

Wang Dong: Security checks are aimed at protecting the safety of passengers and preventing terrorist attacks and destruction.

Passenger: I see. Thank you.

Wang Dong: My pleasure. Have a nice day.

Activity 2: Listen again and try to fill in the blanks.

1. Everyone must _____ a security check, including their luggages.

2. Please _____ your bag _____ and _____ it _____ the X-ray machine.

Activity 3: Work in pairs.

Practice the dialogue with your partner.

Activity 4: Role play.

Dialogue with given words.

Words and Phrases You May Use

luggage   attack   protect   prevent   a bottle of water

Words and Phrases

rule	[ruːl]	n.	统治；规则	What's wrong?			怎么了？
conveyor	[kən'veɪə(r)]	n.	传送带	security	[sɪ'kjʊərəti]	n.	安全
belt	[belt]	n.	带；腰带；地带	prevent	[prɪ'vent]	v.	阻止；防止；预防
screen	[skriːn]	vt.	筛查	terrorist	['terərɪst]	adj.	恐怖的
X-ray	['eksreɪ]	n.	X射线；X射线照片	go through			通过
strict	[strɪkt]	adj.	严格的	security check			安检

Scene: On Monday morning, two young men are passing the security check. The security inspector asks them to open the luggage for inspection, and Lily helps them on the side.

Dialogue B   Please Open Your Luggage for Inspection

Activity 5: Think and answer.

1. Why does the security inspector ask the two young men to open their luggage?
_____

2. What can't be taken on in the subway?
_____

Inspector: Hello! Please open your luggage for inspection.

Passenger 1: Ah. Why would I open the luggage?

Inspector: Let's check it if there are some prohibited items that cannot be taken on the subway.

(As the young man is opening his luggage, Lily is explaining to them.)

Lily: Sir, the subway regulations prohibit carrying more than 350 mL gel on the subway, and the hair gel in your luggage is 500 mL. Hair gel is a flammable and explosive substance.

Passenger 2: Sorry, we didn't even know before.

Lily: It's Okay.

Passenger 1: What else can't I take on the subway?

Lily: Any weapons, aggressive tools, ammunition and flammable, explosive, radioactive, toxic, corrosive or other items are strictly prohibited from being carried on the subway.

Passengers: I see. Thanks a lot.

Lily: My pleasure. Thank you for your cooperation.

Activity 6: Listen again and try to tick the right sentences according to dialogue B.

(   ) 1. Passengers can only get on the subway after security check.

(   ) 2. There are some firecrackers in their luggage.

(　　) 3. Passengers cannot carry any weapons on the subway.

Activity 7: Work in pairs.

Practice the dialogue with your partner.

Activity 8: Role play.

Dialogue with given words.

Words and Phrases You May Use

luggage　　flammable　　mL　　gel　　tool　　item

Words and Phrases

substance	['sʌbstəns]	n.	物品	corrosive	[kə'rəʊsɪv]	adj.	腐蚀的
tool	[tuːl]	n.	工具	mL (milliliter)	['mɪlɪˌliːtər]	n.	毫升
inspection	[ɪn'spekʃ(ə)n]	n.	检查	gel	[dʒel]	n.	凝胶；胶体
flammable	['flæməb(ə)l]	adj.	易燃的	weapon	['wepən]	n.	武器
explosive	[ɪk'spləʊsɪv]	adj.	爆炸性的	aggressive	[ə'gresɪv]	adj.	侵略性的
ammunition	[ˌæmjə'nɪʃ(ə)n]	n.	弹药	item	['aɪtəm]	n.	物品
radioactive	[ˌreɪdiəʊ'æktɪv]	adj.	有辐射的	luggage	['lʌgɪdʒ]	n.	行李
toxic	['tɒksɪk]	adj.	有毒的	prohibit	[prə'hɪbɪt]	vt.	阻止；禁止

Knowledge Expansion

1. The security inspector will conduct a security check on you.
   安检人员将对您进行安全检查。
2. You can take them back after going through the security gate.
   通过安检门之后，您可以把它们取回。
3. It depends.
   看情况而定。
4. The X-ray machine won't damage the laptop.
   X射线设备对笔记本电脑没有伤害。
5. You can go now.
   你们现在可以走了。
6. Please take all of your belongings with you.
   请带上您的所有物品。
7. Please open it for a further check.
   请打开，我们要进一步检查。
8. Could you please open it and take a sip?
   请您打开喝一口，可以吗？

9. They are not permitted to be taken on the subway.
   这些物品不允许被带上地铁。

Exercise 1

Choose Proper Words to Fill in the Blanks

1. What's _____? (on/wrong)
2. I don't know why you're so _____. (street/strict)
3. Could you please open it and take a _____. (sap/sip)
4. What else can't I take _____ the subway? (on/to)
5. The security inspector will conduct a _____ check on you. (security/ luggage)
6. It _____. (depends/depend)
7. Please take all of your _____ with you. (belongs/belongings)
8. Please open it for a _____ check. (far/further)
9. They are not _____ to be taken on the subway. (permitted/permit)

Exercise 2

Translate the Following Sentences into English

1. 请接受安检。
2. 请把您的行李放在传送带上并通过X射线设备。
3. 安检是为了什么？
4. 让我们检查一下是否有禁止被带上地铁的物品。
5. 地铁规定禁止携带超过350毫升的凝胶上车。
6. 安检人员将对您进行安全检查。
7. 视情况而定。
8. 请带上您的所有物品。
9. 请打开它，我们要进一步检查。
10. 这些物品不允许被带上地铁。

Reading and Writing

Security Check in the Subway

As you know, subway is one of the most convenient transportation. Safety is more important for the subway because it runs in a relatively enclosed space. Any small negligence may lead to a catastrophe. So, some things can't be carried on the subway.

It is strictly prohibited to carry inflammable and explosive, toxic, corrosive, radioactive and antipersonnel items, such as the detonator, firecrackers, gasoline, diesel, kerosene, paint, liquefied gas, aggressive tools and various acids, and other items endangering public security.

It is forbidden to carry items of overlength (more than 1.8 meters), fragile (such as glass and glass products, etc.) or heavy (such as bicycles, washing machines, TVs, refrigerators). The articles that interfere with the vehicle traffic and public health, and animals can't be taken on the subway.

The security inspectors will check in different ways according to different situations, for example, check with X-ray equipment or portable scanners and even with the help of police dogs.

Words and Phrases

relatively	[ˈrelətɪvli]	adv.	相对地	enclosed	[ɪnˈkləʊzd]	adj.	封闭的
acid	[ˈæsɪd]	n.	酸	negligence	[ˈneɡlɪdʒəns]	n.	疏忽
endanger	[ɪnˈdeɪndʒə(r)]	vt.	危及	catastrophe	[kəˈtæstrəfi]	n.	灾难
overlength	[ˈəʊvəleŋθ]	adj.	超长的	antipersonnel	[ˌæntɪˌpɜːsəˈnel]	adj.	杀伤的
product	[ˈprɒdʌkt]	n.	产品	detonator	[ˈdetəneɪtə(r)]	n.	雷管；炸药
refrigerator	[rɪˈfrɪdʒəreɪtə(r)]	n.	冰箱	firecracker	[ˈfaɪəkrækə(r)]	n.	鞭炮
interfere	[ˌɪntəˈfɪə(r)]	vi.	干涉；妨碍	gasoline	[ˈɡæsəliːn]	n.	汽油
portable	[ˈpɔːtəb(ə)l]	adj.	便携式的	diesel	[ˈdiːz(ə)l]	n.	柴油
scanner	[ˈskænə(r)]	n.	扫描仪；扫描器	kerosene	[ˈkerəsiːn]	n.	煤油
liquefied	[ˈlɪkwɪfaɪd]	adj.	液化的	paint	[peɪnt]	n.	油漆

Activity 9: Read and answer.

1. Why do more and more people prefer to travel by subway?

_____

2. Can you take any firecrackers on the subway?

_____

3. Can you smoke in a carriage or in a station?
_____

4. Which one can a passenger take on the subway, TV, bicycle or handbag?
_____

Activity 10: Read and write (Read the following paragraphs and fill in the blanks with proper words).

| choice | various | police dog | overlength | environment |
| firecrackers | convenience | important | portable | accept |

Accept Security Check Consciously

Beijing subway has developed rapidly in recent years. Nowadays, traveling by subway is the first _____ for many people because of its _____. In morning-evening rush hours, so many people influx into subway stations with _____ kinds of luggage. So, safety becomes more and more _____. We should _____ security check consciously for creating a favorable _____. We should not take these things on the subway, such as _____, gasoline, aggressive tools and some _____ items. In some main stations, if you have some liquid with you, such as a bottle of water, you have to open it and take a sip. And you should even accept the security check with a _____ scanner or a _____. By the way, the X-ray machine won't damage your luggage.

Communicative Activity

Discuss the following topics in groups of five.

Topic 1: Mr. Smith is going to take the subway. You remind him that there are two lighters in his bag, but he is unwilling to throw them away. How can you persuade him?

Topic 2: Bob is traveling in Beijing for sightseeing. Today, he's stopped by the subway security inspector because of a bottle of water in his handbag.

Self-Check

I can speak and write:

☐ security   ☐ scanner   ☐ flammable   ☐ explosive
☐ strictly   ☐ prohibit   ☐ radioactive ☐ toxic
☐ corrosive   ☐ gasoline   ☐ diesel   ☐ paint
☐ acid   ☐ interfere ☐ overlength   ☐ portable

I can translate these sentences into Chinese:

☐ 1. Security check, please.
☐ 2. Please put your bag on the conveyor belt and pass it through the X-ray machine.
☐ 3. Could you please open it and take a sip?
☐ 4. Security checks are aimed at protecting the safety of passengers.
☐ 5. Let's check it if there are some prohibited items that cannot be taken on the subway.
☐ 6. Any weapons, aggressive tools, ammunition and flammable, explosive, radioactive, toxic, corrosive or other items are strictly prohibited from being carried on the subway.
☐ 7. Any small negligence may lead to a catastrophe.
☐ 8. The security inspectors will check in different ways according to different situations.

I can:

☐ explain the importance of security checks to passengers.
☐ tell passengers how to undergo security checks.

Complementary Reading

Understanding Subway Security Checks-Ensuring Safe Journeys

Subway systems around the world prioritize passenger safety, and one crucial aspect of this is the implementation of security checks. These measures aim to maintain a secure environment for commuters and prevent potential threats. Let's learn about the purposes and processes of subway security checks.

(1) Purposes of Subway Security Checks: The primary goal of subway security checks is to ensure the safety of all passengers and minimize potential risks. By examining luggage, handbags and personal belongings, authorities can identify prohibited items that may jeopardize the safety and well-being of commuters. This thorough screening helps maintain a secure environment within the subway network.

(2) Prohibited Items: To enhance safety, there are specific items that are generally

not allowed in subway stations and trains. These include weapons or objects that could potentially harm others, such as firearms, sharp objects, explosive materials, and flammable liquids. Additionally, substances that could endanger public health and safety, like illegal drugs or hazardous chemicals, are strictly prohibited.

(3) Security Check Processes:

a) X-ray Scanning: In most cases, security checkpoints include X-ray scanners for bags. Passengers are required to place their bags on a conveyor belt for inspection. The X-ray scans help identify any suspicious items or potential threats hidden within luggage.

b) Metal Detectors: To detect metallic objects, such as knives or firearms, passengers walk through metal detectors. These devices emit electromagnetic fields and can identify metallic items that may be concealed on a person's body. If the metal detector is triggered, further examination or secondary screening may be necessary.

c) Handheld Scanners: Occasionally, security personnel might use handheld scanners to conduct additional screenings. These scanners emit low-energy radio waves to identify metallic or electronic objects that may have been missed during the initial screening.

(4) Cooperation and Etiquette:During security checks, cooperation from passengers is essential. It is advisable to:

- Follow instructions provided by security personnel.
- Be prepared to remove jackets, belts and shoes, if requested.
- Keep electronic devices readily accessible for inspection.
- Inform security personnel about medical implants or any specific concerns in advance.

Subway security checks are vital for ensuring safe journeys for all passengers. By implementing strict measures, authorities can deter potential threats and maintain a secure environment within the subway system. As commuters, it is our collective responsibility to cooperate with these protocols, contributing to the overall safety and well-being of everyone on the subway.

城市轨道交通客运服务英语
（第3版）

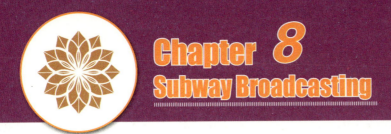

Chapter 8
Subway Broadcasting

Objectives

1. Knowledge: Learn the vocabularies and sentences of subway broadcasting.
2. Ability: Be able to conduct subway broadcasting.
3. Morality: Provide accurate and meticulous services for passengers.

Suggested Class Hours

4 class hours

Warm-up

Have you ever paid attention to subway broadcasting? Talk to your classmates about the subway broadcasting you have heard.

Listening and Speaking

Scene: Lily is a new employee of the subway company, responsible for subway broadcasting. She is currently discussing with her colleague Mr. Chen about subway broadcasting.

Dialogue A   How to Broadcast Correctly?

Activity 1: Listen and guess.

1. How to broadcast in dense crowds?

   _____

2. To maintain order, we should broadcast like this:

   _____

Lily: Good morning, Mr. Chen. Would you please do me a favor?

Mr. Chen: Certainly. What's the matter?

Lily: As a new broadcaster, I have some questions to ask you about subway broadcasting.

Mr. Chen: No problem, you can ask.

Lily: How should I remind passengers when there is much subway traffic?

Mr. Chen: Okay, in this situation, you should broadcast like this: "Your attention, please. Crowd Management Plans are now in operation. Please don't wait inside the station. Follow the directions to exit. Thank you for your cooperation."

Lily: Oh, I see. What should I broadcast in order to maintain order?

Mr. Chen: Broadcast like this: "Your attention, please. For safety reasons, please use the elevator if you have baggage or bulky items. Please let passengers exit first and keep clear from the screen doors. Thank you for your cooperation."

Lily: Thanks a lot.

Mr. Chen: My pleasure.

Activity 2: Listen again and try to fill in the blanks.

1. Crowd Management Plans are now _____.
2. Follow _____ to exit.
3. For safety reasons, please use the elevator if you have baggage or _____.

Activity 3: Work in pairs.

Practice the dialogue with your partner.

Activity 4: Role play.

Dialogue with given words.

Words and Phrases You May Use

certainly   broadcast   in operation   remind

Words and Phrases

baggage	['bægɪdʒ]	n.	行李	operation	[ˌɒpə'reɪʃ(ə)n]	n.	操作
bulky	['bʌlki]	adj.	庞大的；笨重的	favor	['feɪvə(r)]	n.	帮助
dense	[dens]	adj.	密集的	cooperation	[kəʊˌɒpə'reɪʃ(ə)n]	n.	合作
certainly	['sɜːt(ə)nli]	adv.	当然	attention	[ə'tenʃ(ə)n]	n.	注意
Crowd Management Plans			限流措施	remind	[rɪ'maɪnd]	vt.	提醒
maintain	[meɪn'teɪn]	vt.	保持，维持				

Scene: Yang Ming is Lily's good friend. He is an English teacher at a university and takes the subway to work every day. They meet on the same train today.

Dialogue B   Subway Broadcasting Should be Cheerful and Clear

Activity 5: Think and answer.

1. What is Yang Ming's suggestions for Lily about subway broadcasting?

_____

2. What is Yang Ming always confused about in China?

_____

(*Broadcasting: Welcome to Subway Line 1. This train is bound for Sihui Dong (E). The next station is Sihui. The door on the left side will be used. Please keep clear of the door. Please get ready for your arrival.*)

  Yang Ming: Hi, Lily. Long time no see. It's amazing to meet you here. How have you been lately?

  Lily: It's okey. And you? I heard you are going to settle in Beijing.

  Yang Ming: Yes. I heard that you work in Beijing subway, what is your position?

(*Broadcasting: To keep a clean and healthy environment, do not eat, drink, smoke or litter on train. Thank you.*)

Lily: I am a subway broadcaster. As an English teacher, could you give me some advice about subway broadcasting?

Yang Ming: Of course, it's my pleasure.

Lily: It's very kind of you. Is the voice broadcast of subway broadcasting too mechanical?

Yang Ming: Yes, there's no emotion at all, and it sounds very cold. I hope the broadcasting tone can be more cheerful, making passengers feel happy and comfortable.

Lily: Anything else?

Yang Ming: Sometimes the announcements in subway broadcasting are very obscure and difficult to understand. Some of the words are too professional and difficult to understand. I hope they can use simpler and clear languages to make it easier for passengers to understand.

Lily: OK, it's a good suggestion. Thank you.

(*Broadcasting: The next station is Sihui Dong (E). Please get ready for your arrival, and make sure you have all your belongings with you. Sihui Dong (E) is a transfer station. Passengers for the Batong Line, please prepare to get off.*)

The train stops. (*We are arriving at Sihui Dong (E). Welcome to take this line on your next trip. Have a nice day.*)

Activity 6: Listen again and try to fill in the blanks.

1. The door on the left side will be _____. Please keep _____ of the door.
2. I hope they can use _____ and _____ languages to take it easier for passengers to understand.

Activity 7: Work in pairs.

Practice the dialogue with your partner.

Activity 8: Role play.

Dialogue with given words.

Words and Phrases You May Use

station   arrive   keep   clear   transfer   get ready for

Words and Phrases

be bound for			开往	environment [ɪnˈvaɪrənmənt]	n. 环境
belongings	[bɪˈlɒŋɪŋz]	n.	财产，财物	settle [ˈset(ə)l]	vi. 解决；定居
transfer	[trænsˈfɜː(r)]	n.	换乘	litter [ˈlɪtə(r)]	vi. 乱扔废弃物
arrival	[əˈraɪv(ə)l]	n.	到来，到达	trip [trɪp]	n 旅行

Knowledge Expansion

1. The next station is Haidian Huangzhuang. Haidian Huangzhuang is a transfer station. Passengers for Line 4, please prepare to get off.
   列车运行前方是海淀黄庄站，海淀黄庄站是换乘站，换乘地铁4号线的乘客请做好下车准备。
2. Welcome to Subway Line 10. The terminal station is Bagou.
   欢迎乘坐地铁10号线列车。本次列车终点站是巴沟站。
3. We are arriving at Suzhou Jie station.
   列车到达苏州街站。
4. This train to Sihui will not stop at Tian'anmendong.
   本次开往四惠方向的列车将在天安门东站通过不停车。
5. The train is departing. Please stand clear from the screen doors.
   列车即将出站，请勿倚靠屏蔽门。
6. Train service for today has ended. Please leave the station.
   今天的列车服务已经结束，请尽快出站。
7. Thank you for choosing Beijing Subway Line 2.
   感谢您选择搭乘北京地铁2号线。
8. The train for Songjiazhuang is the last train. Please board immediately.
   本次列车是开往宋家庄方向的末班车，请尽快上车。
9. Please wait in line while passengers exit from the train.
   请排队候车，先下后上。
10. Please take care of your children and belongings. Thank you for your cooperation.
    请照顾好您的小孩，保管好随身携带的物品。谢谢合作。

Exercise 1

Choose Proper Words to Fill in the Blanks

1. Would you please do me a _____? (favor/fever)
2. What's the _____? (wrong/matter)
3. Crowd Management Plans are now _____ operation. (at/in)
4. Follow the directions to _____. (exit/out)
5. This train is bound _____ Sihui Dong (E). (for/on)
6. Please get ready for your _____. (arrival/arrive)
7. Please keep _____ of the door. (clean/clear)
8. Make sure you have all your belongings _____ you. (with/of)
9. Welcome to take this line _____ your next trip. (on/in)

Exercise 2

Translate the Following Sentences into English

1. 今天的列车服务已经结束，请尽快出站。
2. 本站正采取限流措施。
3. 为了您和他人的安全，请携带大件行李的乘客使用升降电梯。
4. 本次列车开往四惠东。
5. 请您准备下车。
6. 列车即将出站，请勿倚靠车门。
7. 列车将开启左侧车门。
8. 欢迎您乘坐地铁1号线。
9. 请排队下车，先下后上。
10. 感谢您选择搭乘北京地铁2号线。

Reading and Writing

Your Attention, Please

"Your attention, please. The train is arriving. This train is bound for Sihui. Please mind the gap between the train and the platform. For your safety, please stand back from the platform screen doors. Please move along the platform to the middle of the train for easier boarding. To keep a clean and healthy environment, don't smoke or litter on trains or in stations. Please wait in line and take care of your children and belongings while passengers exit from the train. For safety reasons, please use our elevators if you have baggage or bulky items. When using the escalators, please stand firmly and hold the handrail. Please don't run or walk in the wrong direction. Please offer your seat to someone in need. Thank you for your cooperation. We hope you have a pleasant journey."

Words and Phrases

smoke	[sməʊk]	vt.	抽烟	gap	[gæp]	n.	间隙；缺口
reason	['riːz(ə)n]	n.	理由	pleasant	['plez(ə)nt]	adj.	令人愉快的
handrail	['hændreɪl]	n.	扶手	firm	[fɜːm]	adj.	稳固的
journey	['dʒɜːni]	n.	旅行，旅程	take care of			照顾；注意

Activity 9: Read and answer.

1. Where is the train bound for?
   _____

2. Can you stand near the screen doors when you are waiting for a train?
   _____

3. What should you do if you have baggage or bulky items?
   _____

Activity 10: Read and write (Read the following paragraphs and fill in the blanks with proper words).

| arrival | side | departs | prepare | leaves |
| bound | transfer | keep clear | litter | offer |

Broadcasting in the Subway

Welcome to Subway Line 6. This train is _____ for Haidian Wuluju. The first train _____ Caofang at 5:15. The last train _____ at 23:06. To keep a clean and healthy environment, don't smoke or _____ on trains or in stations. Please _____ your seat to someone in need. Thank you for your cooperation. The next station is Hujialou. Please get ready for your _____. Hujialou is a _____ station. Passengers for Line 10, please _____ to get off. The door on the left _____ will be used. Please _____ of the door. Today is the Mid-autumn Festival. Beijing Subway wish you a happy day!

Communicative Activity

Discuss the following topics in groups of five.

Topic 1: One day, some passengers were stranded on the platform due to a power outage, fearing that the subway would be delayed and the station facilities at the subway station would be unable to operate. If you are a subway broadcaster on duty. How would you broadcast?

Topic 2: If you are a subway broadcaster on duty, how should you broadcast to remind passengers to maintain order? Please use the words and sentences learned in this lesson.

Self-Check

I can speak and write:

- [ ] employee
- [ ] attention
- [ ] suggestion
- [ ] pleasure
- [ ] broadcaster
- [ ] direction
- [ ] cooperation
- [ ] advice
- [ ] delay
- [ ] belongings
- [ ] broadcast
- [ ] gap
- [ ] arrival
- [ ] be bound for
- [ ] firm
- [ ] handrail

I can translate these sentences into Chinese:

- [ ] 1. Your attention, please.
- [ ] 2. Welcome to Subway Line 10.
- [ ] 3. Please get ready for your arrival.
- [ ] 4. The door on the left Side will be used.
- [ ] 5. Please keep clear of the door.
- [ ] 6. Haidian Huangzhuang is a transfer station. Passengers for Line 4, please prepare to get off.
- [ ] 7. When using the escalators, please stand firmly and hold the handrail.
- [ ] 8. Please offer your seat to someone in need.

I can:

- [ ] provide passengers with the services they need in subway.
- [ ] broadcast in English on the subway.

Complementary Reading

Effective Strategies for Subway Announcers to Excel in Their Role

As an essential component of commuters experience, subway announcers play a critical role in ensuring a smooth and efficient transportation system. Their clear and concise announcements provide vital information to passengers, helping them navigate the intricate webs of underground networks. This article outlines some effective strategies that subway announcers can employ to excel in their profession.

(1) Speak clearly and audibly

One of the primary responsibilities of a subway announcer is to convey information effectively. Speak slowly, pronounce words clearly, and ensure that your voice is audible throughout the station and train. A well-projected voice allows passengers to understand important updates and directions without confusion or frustration.

(2) Use standardized language

To maintain consistency and clarity, subway announcers should adhere to a standardized language when making announcements. Using universally understood terms and phrases helps avoid barriers caused by different languages or dialects. It is essential to strike a balance between being informative and concise while avoiding excessive jargon.

(3) Provide timely updates

An effective subway announcer keeps passengers informed with accurate and timely updates. Whether it's announcing delays, service interruptions, or conveying essential safety information, ensure that your announcements are up-to-date. In situations where there may be significant disruptions, be proactive in providing alternative routes or transportation options.

(4) Display empathy and professionalism

Subway journeys can sometimes be stressful or frustrating for passengers. Exhibiting empathy and a professional demeanor help build a positive rapport with commuters. While addressing delays or inconveniences, acknowledge passengers' concerns, offer reassurance, and provide estimated timelines for resolution. A compassionate and composed approach can go a long way in fostering passenger satisfaction.

(5) Adapt to changing circumstances

As a subway announcer, you will encounter various unexpected situations such as emergencies, security alerts, or customer service issues. It is crucial to adapt quickly and respond appropriately. In emergency scenarios, follow established protocols for evacuation or other necessary actions, while maintaining a calm and confident demeanor.

(6) Seek feedback and self-improvement opportunities

Constantly seek feedback from passengers, colleagues, and supervisors regarding your performance. This feedback can provide valuable insights into areas that need improvement or refinement. Additionally, consider attending workshops, courses, or training sessions to enhance communication skills or develop expertise in specific ar eas, such as emergency management or public address systems.

The role of a subway announcer is indispensable in ensuring a safe, efficient, and enjoyable commuting experience for passengers. By employing effective strategies such as clear communication, standardized language, timely updates, empathy, adaptability, and continuous self-improvement, subway announcers can excel in their profession. Remember, the goal is to create an environment where passengers feel informed, supported, and confident in their subway journey.

Chapter 9
Handle Lost Items

Objectives

1. Knowledge: Learn the vocabularies and sentences for handling lost items at subway stations.
2. Ability: Can help passengers handle lost items.
3. Morality: Handle the issues of lost items for passengers with patience and warmth.

Suggested Class Hours

4 class hours

Warm-up

Lily works at the lost and found office in the subway. There are many items left by passengers in the subway, such as umbrellas, phones, keys, tickets, wallets, etc. What other things can you think of the passengers have lost on the subway?

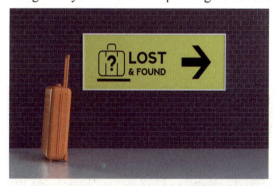

Listening and Speaking

Scene: Lily works at the lost and found office in the subway when the phone rings. Let's see what exactly happened.

Dialogue A   When and Where Did Your Briefcase Get Lost?

Activity 1: Listen and guess.

1. What did the passenger lose?

_____

2. Who should passengers turn to for help?

_____

Lily: This is the lost and found office. What can I do for you?

Passenger: Yes, please. I lost my briefcase.

Lily: Can you tell me more information about the briefcase?

Passenger: Well, The briefcase is light brown with two buckles on the front.

Lily: What is in the briefcase?

Passenger: Some important documents, pens and a book.

Lily: OK. When and where did your briefcase get lost?

Passenger: Well, At around 5:10 p.m., When I went to the restroom at the back of the station to wash my hands, I placed it on the sink.

Lily: OK. Please leave your contact information.

Passenger: My name is Wang Gang, and my phone number is 635349X.

Lily: Fine. Don't worry. We will send someone to find it immediately and notify you as soon as there is any news.

Passenger: Thanks a lot.

Lily: My pleasure.

Activity 2: Listen again and try to fill in the blanks.

1. Can you tell me more _____ about the briefcase?

2. _____ and _____ did your briefcase get lost?

Activity 3: Work in pairs.

Practice the dialogue with your partner.

Activity 4: Role play.

Dialogue with given words.

Words and Phrases You May Use

lost and found office	briefcase	buckle	document	contact
light	sink	phone	front	

Words and Phrases

document	['dɒkjumənt]	n.	文件	briefcase	['briːfkeɪs]	n.	公文包
phone	[fəʊn]	n.	电话	buckle	['bʌk(ə)l]	n.	扣；扣带
contact information			联系方式	sink	[sɪŋk]	n.	洗手台

Scene: Lily works at the lost and found office. A passenger hears that there is a lost and found message on the radio. He is coming to see if it's his lost wallet.

Dialogue B   Could You Tell Me What Your Wallet Looks Like?

Activity 5: Think and answer.

1. What did the passenger lose?

_____

2. How does Lily deal with the problem?

_____

Lily: Hello, sir. What can I do for you?

Passenger: I just heard that there was a lost and found message on the radio. I come to see if it's my lost wallet.

Lily: Take a seat please. Could you tell me what your wallet looks like?

Passenger: Of course. The wallet is black and leather.

Lily: Is there a zipper on the wallet?

Passenger: No, the wallet is opened and closed with a button.

Lily: Is there anything special about your wallet?

Passenger: Yes. The logo of Polo is located in the bottom right corner of the wallet.

Lily: OK, can you tell me what is in the wallet?

Passenger: Well, some cash and two bank cards.

Lily: After confirmation, this is your wallet. After filling in the lost and found form, you can take it back. Thank you for your cooperation.

Passenger: OK. Thank you so much.

Lily: You are welcome.

Activity 6: Listen again and try to fill in the blanks.

1. Could you tell me what your wallet _____ like?
2. After filling in the lost and found form, you can _____ it back.

Activity 7: Work in pairs.
Practice the dialogue with your partner.

Activity 8: Role play.
Dialogue with given words.

Words and Phrases You May Use

bank card   take back   logo   button   form   lost and found

Words and Phrases

leather	['leðə(r)]	n.	皮，皮革	zipper	['zɪpə(r)]	n.	拉链
button	['bʌt(ə)n]	n.	纽扣	form	[fɔːm]	n.	表，表格
radio	['reɪdiəʊ]	n.	广播	logo	['ləʊgəʊ]	n.	商标

Knowledge Expansion

1. I need some details clearly.
   我需要一些具体的信息。
2. Tell me what it looks like, first of all.
   首先告诉我它是什么样子的。
3. Does it have any other distinguishing features?
   它还有其他明显的特征吗?
4. What is in the briefcase?
   公文包里有什么呢?
5. Please leave your contact information.
   请留下您的联系方式。
6. Can you leave a contact number?

能留个联系电话吗?

7. Take a seat please, sir.

先生，请坐。

8. Can you tell me what is in it?

您能说出里面有哪些东西吗?

9. Before you get it back, please sign and confirm on the lost and found form.

在您拿回去之前，请在失物招领表上签字确认。

10. It's our responsibility.

这是我们的责任。

Exercise 1

Choose Proper Words to Fill in the Blanks

1. Could you tell me what your wallet _____ like? (look/looks)
2. Can you tell me what is _____ the wallet? (in/on)
3. Can you _____ a contact number? (leave/left)
4. We will send someone to find it immediately and notify you as _____ as there is any news. (soon/far)
5. Can you leave a _____ number? (contact/address)
6. Take a _____ please. (see/seat)
7. I need some _____ clearly. (detail/details)
8. After _____, this is your wallet. (confirm/confirmation)
9. Before you get it back, please sign and _____ on the lost and found form. (confirmation/confirm)

Exercise 2

Translate the Following Sentences into English

1. 先生，请坐。
2. 这是我们的责任。
3. 您能告诉我您的钱包长什么样子吗?
4. 公文包里有什么呢?
5. 请留下您的联系方式。
6. 钱包有拉链吗?
7. 在您拿回去之前，请在失物招领表上签字确认。
8. 我们会立刻派人去找，有任何消息立即通知您。
9. 它还有其他明显的特征吗?

10. 我需要一些具体的信息。

Reading and Writing

Steps for Handling General Lost Items

When the passenger hands in lost property to the station, the station staff must check the lost items carefully and clearly with the passenger and fill in the "Lost and Found" form in detail, including the name of the items, the features, the time and place that the passenger found the lost property.

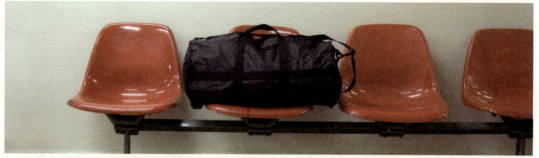

Paste the lost property tag

According to the subway company's regulation rules, the station staff must fill in the "Lost and Found" form and paste the tag on the items.

Contact and keep

If the station staff can find the owner's information, he/she should contact the owner immediately. Otherwise, keep the lost property properly.

Unclaimed items

If no owner claims the lost items that day, the station should transfer the lost property to the lost and found office.

Words and Phrases

general	['dʒen(ə)rəl]	adj.	一般的	paste	[peɪst]	vt.	粘贴
tag	[tæg]	n.	标签	properly	['prɒpəli]	adv.	妥善地
fill in			填写	hand in			上交
in detail			详细地				

Activity 9: Read and answer.

1. How to handle the lost property that other passengers pick up?

   _____

2. Where would the items be transferred if no owner

claims them that day at the station?

_____

Activity 10: Read and write (Read the following paragraphs and fill in the blanks with proper words).

> ensure   allowed   abandoned   properly   In addition

How to Handle the Abandoned Items Which Seem Dangerous?

Lily comes to the station master to talk about the abandoned luggage. The station master tells Lily patiently: "To _____ the normal operation of the train as well as the safety of passengers and their properties, the following items will not be _____ aboard:

"Item weighting over 20kg; with a length (sun of length, width and height) exceeding 1.8m, and a volume exceeding 0.15m³ is not allowed to be carried. _____ , inflammable, explosive or dangerous goods and prohibited articles are not allowed into subway stations. If anyone bears witness to someone else carrying inflammable, explosive or dangerous goods, it is encouraged to report the offence at once. If passengers find any suspicious _____ luggage or items at the station or in the carriage, you should tell them not to open it. You just contact the police or they can report the items to the station or dial 110 immediately. The police and the subway management company will deal with it _____."

Communicative Activity

Discuss the following topics in groups of five.

Topic 1: Xiao Wang called the lost and found office in the subway. There is an unclaimed luggage on the platform that makes a strange noise. Can you tell him what to do?

Topic 2: Miley is an international student, she lost her laptop on the subway. How can we help her take it back?

Self-Check

I can speak and write:

☐ property   ☐ form   ☐ sign   ☐ cooperation
☐ contact   ☐ feature   ☐ zipper   ☐ properly
☐ leather   ☐ buckle   ☐ logo   ☐ general

I can translate these sentences into Chinese:

☐ 1. Tell me what it looks like.
☐ 2. Can you tell me what is in it?
☐ 3. I need some details clearly.
☐ 4. We will send someone to find it immediately and notify you as soon as there is any news.
☐ 5. Does it have any other distinguishing features?
☐ 6. The wallet is opened and closed with a button.
☐ 7. After filling in the lost and found form, you can take it back.
☐ 8. When and where did your briefcase get lost?
☐ 9. It's our responsibility.

I can:

☐ help passengers find lost items in the subway.
☐ tell passengers how to handle the abandoned items properly.

Complementary Reading

Meeting Point

In order to facilitate the quick reunion of the passengers who get separated, some subway stations set up the meeting point.

If you accidentally pass by a friend or a family member at the subway station, a small meeting point can help you quickly locate each other in the station.

Chapter 10
Handle Complaints

🌾 Objectives

1. Knowledge: Learn the vocabularies and sentences for handling complaints in the subway.
2. Ability: Effectively handle passenger complaints.
3. Morality: Handle complaints calmly and skillfully.

🌾 Suggested Class Hours

4 class hours

🌾 Warm-up

Although Lily and Wang Dong work hard in their respective positions in the subway, there are still complaints from passengers who are not satisfied with their services. Can you think of what passengers would complain about?

Listening and Speaking

Scene: Lily is puzzled by the recent customer complaints that she receives recently. Mrs. Zhang helps her and gives her some advice.

Dialogue A   I Believe You Can Handle It Well

Activity 1: Listen and guess.
1. Why does Lily look so sad?
_____
2. How to effectively handle passenger complaints?
_____

Mrs. Zhang: You seem unhappy. What is going on?
Lily: Yeah. I'm a bit tired.
Mrs. Zhang: What can I do for you?
Lily: I am unable to respond to the complaints from passengers about subway facility malfunctions.
Mrs. Zhang: Relax, I believe you can handle it well. I have also encountered many complaints from passengers about subway facilities, environment, services, and even unexpected things before.
Lily: Really? Can you give me some advice?
Mrs. Zhang: At this point, we need to take a positive attitude. Firstly, listen carefully and show concern. Secondly, be calm and comfort gently. Thirdly, do a good job of explanation. Fourthly, ensure that passengers are satisfied with our complaint handling results.
Lily: Thank you so much.
Mrs. Zhang: The most important thing is that we should provide assistance to passengers as politely as possible.
Lily: I will. Thanks a lot.
Mrs. Zhang: It's my pleasure. Have a nice day.

Activity 2: Listen again and try to fill in the blanks.
1. Can you give me some _____?
2. We need to take a _____ attitude.

Activity 3: Work in pairs.

Practice the dialogue with your partner.

Activity 4: Role play.

Dialogue with given words.

Words and Phrases You May Use

complain   positive   be calm   handle   assistance   politely

Words and Phrases

customer	['kʌstəmə(r)]	n.	顾客；客户	satisfied	['sætɪsfaɪd]	adj.	满意的
positive	['pɒzətɪv]	adj.	积极的	handle	['hænd(ə)l]	v.	应对；处理
politely	[pə'laɪtli]	adv.	有礼貌地	attitude	['ætɪtjuːd]	n.	态度

Scene: Wang Dong works at the customer service center and is responding to a complaint call from an angry passenger. What exactly happened?

Dialogue B   A Complaint Call from an Angry Passenger

Activity 5: Think and answer.

1. Why does the passenger make phone complaints?
_____

2. What does Wang Dong suggest for passengers to do?
_____

Zhang Wei: Hello, I am Zhang Wei and I have a strong complaint to make.
Wang Dong: Okay, first of all, we apologize for our inadequate service. Sir, could you please explain the situation you have encountered?
Zhang Wei: Yesterday, I bought a yikatong ticket at the ticket office and recharged 100 yuan. I can't pass the gate today. It showed that the balance was insufficient. Next, I went to the ticket office to inquiry, but they didn't help me solve the problem.
Wang Dong: I'm very sorry. I promise that such a thing will never happen again.
Zhang Wei: What should I do now?
Wang Dong: Please come to the station with your ticket. I will check the records and help you update the balance of the ticket.
Zhang Wei: All right.
Wang Dong: Thank you for your call. If you have any further questions, please feel free to call us immediately.
Zhang Wei: Thank you. Bye.
Wang Dong: Bye.

Activity 6: Listen again and try to fill in the blanks.

1. I have a _____ to make.
2. We _____ for our inadequate service.

Activity 7: Work in pairs.

Practice the dialogue with your partner.

Activity 8: Role play.

Dialogue with given words.

Words and Phrases You May Use

situation　　strong　　apologize　　hope　　recharge　　insufficient

Words and Phrases

inadequate	[ɪnˈædɪkwət]	adj.	不充分的，不周到的	insufficient	[ˌɪnsəˈfɪʃ(ə)nt]	adj.	不足的
inquiry	[ɪnˈkwaɪəri]	v.	询问	situation	[ˌsɪtʃuˈeɪʃ(ə)n]	n.	情况
apologize	[əˈpɒlədʒaɪz]	vt.	道歉				

Knowledge Expansion

1. What happened?
   发生什么事了？
2. We should take a positive attitude.
   我们应该采取一种积极的态度。
3. It's my pleasure.
   这是我的荣幸。
4. I'm afraid I have to make a serious complaint.
   恐怕我必须投诉。
5. What seems to be the trouble?
   您有什么麻烦吗？
6. Can you give me some details, Mr. Smith?
   史密斯先生，您能详细说说怎么回事吗？
7. I'm very sorry to hear that, Mr. Smith.
   史密斯先生，听到这件事我感到非常抱歉。
8. I promise that such a thing will never happen again.
   我保证以后不会再发生类似的事情。
9. What do you intend to do about this?
   您打算如何处理这事呢？
10. I'll look into the matter for you.
    我会为您调查此事的。

Exercise 1

Choose Proper Words to Fill in the Blanks

1. I'm a _____ tired. (few/bit)

2. We need to _____ a positive attitude. (have/take)
3. I have a strong complaint to _____. (make/take)
4. If you have any further questions, please feel _____ to call us immediately. (fee/free)
5. I am unable to _____ to the complaints from passengers about subway facility malfunctions. (respond/responded)
6. I will _____ the records and help you update the balance of the ticket. (check/look)
7. We _____ for our inadequate service. (apologizes/apologize)
8. I'll _____ the matter for you. (look into/look to)
9. Fourthly, ensure that passengers are satisfied _____ our complaint handling results. (with/on)

Exercise 2

Translate the Following Sentences into English

1. 发生什么事了？
2. 这是我的荣幸。
3. 我会为您调查此事的。
4. 先生，您能说一下您遇到的情况吗？
5. 首先，我为我们不周到的服务感到抱歉。
6. 我们应该采取一种积极的态度。
7. 您有什么麻烦吗？
8. 我保证以后不会再发生类似的事情。
9. 恐怕我必须投诉。
10. 最重要的事情是我们应该尽可能礼貌地为乘客提供帮助。

Reading and Writing

Communication Skills

Communication is an essential part of work and life. We should offer helpful services for the passengers who are not familiar with subway. Station staff should use standard language, pay attention to the tone of the language, grasp and analyze the psychological needs of passengers.

Show Appreciation

As we all know, time is an extremely precious resource. It's important to be respectful. So you'd better get into the main part of your conversation quickly, and be sure to express your thanks for the other individual's time.

Stay Positive

Taking a positive attitude is good for productive communications. The attitude you take should be constructive rather than negative or complaining. Even though you want to express your concerns, being encouraging and kind is the key of the conversation.

Focus on the Results

It's important to figure out what result you want to have before you start the conversation. Knowing your objective helps you lead conversation to the right direction and get the result you want.

Always try to end your communication in a friendly manner. We need to have a good conversation to help us resolve the problems or promote relationships between people. Productive communication involves respects, considerations, awareness and clarity. We should try to have a direct and kind conversation with good results.

Words and Phrases

communication	[kəˌmjuːnɪˈkeɪʃ(ə)n]	n.	交流	pay attention to			注意
conversation	[ˌkɒnvəˈseɪʃ(ə)n]	n.	谈话	essential	[ɪˈsenʃ(ə)l]	adj.	必要的
precious	[ˈpreʃəs]	adj.	宝贵的	psychological	[ˌsaɪkəˈlɒdʒɪk(ə)l]	adj.	心理的
respect	[rɪˈspekt]	n.	尊重	constructive	[kənˈstrʌktɪv]	adj.	建设性的
objective	[əbˈdʒektɪv]	n.	目标	productive	[prəˈdʌktɪv]	adj.	富有成效的
clarity	[ˈklærəti]	n.	清楚；明晰	positive attitude			积极的态度

Activity 9: Read and answer.

1. What communication skills are mentioned in the text?

_____

2. What attitude should you take if you have to handle complaints?

_____

Activity 10: Read and write (Read the following paragraphs and fill in the blanks with proper words).

calm	action	solved	inform
apologize	note	concern	satisfied

The Steps for Handling Passenger Complaints

1. Listen carefully and show your _____.
2. Stay _____ and rational. Never argue with the passengers. Never try to explain yourself.
3. _____ to the passengers for what happened.
4. Take _____ whenever necessary.
5. _____ the passengers what you are going to do and when you will do it or offer an alternative (选择).
6. Take _____ immediately. Refer to your superior (上级) right away whenever necessary.
7. Follow up to make sure the problem is _____.
8. Ask the passengers to make sure that they are _____ with the result.

Communicative Activity

Discuss the following topics in groups of five.

Topic 1: During peak hours, the ticket seller was selling tickets. Smith is a foreigner, jumped a queue to the window and said that his ticket could not pass through the gate. The ticket seller stopped selling tickets and dealt with Smith's problem. Passengers queuing up to buy tickets complained. How do you handle their complaints?

Topic 2: It's raining outside. The water on the umbrellas of passengers entering the station wetted the subway floor, and an old woman slipped and complained that there were no antislip signs at the subway station. How do you respond to her complaint?

Self-Check

I can speak and write:

☐ handle　　　　　☐ customer　　　　☐ look into　　　　☐ malfunction
☐ assure　　　　　☐ satisfied　　　　☐ serious　　　　　☐ immediately
☐ pay attention to　☐ positive　　　　☐ attitude

I can translate these sentences into Chinese:

☐ 1. What happened?
☐ 2. What seems to be the trouble?
☐ 3. Can you give me some advice?
☐ 4. I promise that such a thing will never happen again.
☐ 5. I'm afraid I have to make a serious complaint.
☐ 6. I'll look into the matter for you.
☐ 7. I'm very sorry to hear that.
☐ 8. Can you give me some details?
☐ 9. What do you intend to do about this?
☐ 10. We should take a positive attitude.

I can:

☐ handle complaints calmly and skillfully.
☐ provide assistance to passengers as politely as possible.

Complementary Reading

Handling Passenger Complaints in the Subway

Complaints are an inevitable part of any public transportation system, and the subway is not an exception. As a subway staff, it is our responsibility to address and resolve these complaints efficiently and effectively. Here's a guide on how to handle passenger complaints in the subway:

(1) Listen attentively: When a passenger approaches you with a complaint, give them your full attention. Maintain eye contact and nod occasionally to show that you are listening actively. Encourage them to express their concerns fully without interruption.

(2) Remain calm and empathetic: It is essential to stay calm and composed, regardless of the nature or tone of the complaint. Remember that the passengers may be frustrated or upset, and it is important to empathize with their feelings.

(3) Apologize sincerely: Regardless of fault, offer a sincere apology to the passengers for any inconvenience or discomfort they may have experienced. This gesture shows that you take their complaints seriously and care about their satisfaction genuinely.

(4) Gather relevant information: Ask the passengers for specific details about the incidents to ensure you have a clear understanding of the issues. Document important information, such as the time, date, subway line, and any other relevant details that might be necessary for resolving the complaint.

(5) Offer solutions: Based on the nature of the complaints, provide the passengers with appropriate solutions or alternatives. This might include offering refunds, suggesting

alternative routes, or providing additional assistance. If the complaint requires further investigation, assure the passengers that you will look into the matter promptly.

(6) Follow up: Once the complaint has been resolved, follow up with the passengers to ensure their satisfaction. This can be done through a phone call or email, where you can acknowledge their complaints again, explain the actions taken to rectify the issues, and thank them for bringing it to your attention.

(7) Learn from the complaint: Every complaint is an opportunity for improvement. Analyze the complaints and identify any recurring issues or patterns that could be addressed to enhance the subway's overall performance and passenger experience.

Remember, the subway is a shared space, and it is our duty to provide a safe and comfortable journey for all passengers. By handling complaints promptly and professionally, we can foster a positive environment and improve the overall subway experience for everyone involved.

城市轨道交通客运服务英语
（第3版）

Chapter 11
Cope with High Passenger Flows

🌾 Objectives

1. Knowledge: Learn the vocabularies and sentences for coping with high passenger flows.
2. Ability: Be able to quickly cope with high passenger flows in the subway.
3. Morality: In the face of unexpected situations, be fearless and fulfill your mission.

🌅 Suggested Class Hours

4 class hours

🌱 Warm-up

Look at the following two pictures and talk about your understanding of the high passenger flows in the subway.

🌾 Listening and Speaking

Scene: Due to the high flows of people at Datunludong station, Wang Dong is assisting incoming passengers in evacuating the subway station.

Dialogue A Datunludong Station Is Closed

Activity 1: Listen and guess.

1. Why is the station closed?
   _____
2. What should the passengers do?
   _____

Wang Dong: Attention, please! This station is about to close. Passengers are requested to leave the station as soon as possible.

Passenger: What happened?

Wang Dong: Don't worry, the flows of people at this station have exceeded the limit. For the safety of passengers, we need to close the station.

Passenger: What should we do now?

Wang Dong: Please follow the instructions on the radio and leave the station in an orderly manner. We apologize for any inconvenience caused.

Passenger: How long will it take to reopen this station?

Wang Dong: I don't know yet, you'd better change to another line or take a bus.

Passenger: I see. Thank you.

Wang Dong: My pleasure.

Activity 2: Listen again and try to fill in the blanks.

1. _____, please!
2. Please follow the _____ on the _____ .
3. We apologize for any _____ caused.

Activity 3: Work in pairs.

Practice the dialogue with your partner.

Activity 4: Role play.

Dialogue with given words.

Words and Phrases You May Use

attention   change to   take a bus   need to   follow

Words and Phrases

exceed	[ɪk'siːd]	vt.	超过（数量）	flow	[fləʊ]	n.	流；流动
instruction	[ɪn'strʌkʃ(ə)n]	n.	指示	need to			需要；需要做

Scene: In order to evacuate excessive crowds, the station arranged an empty train to pick up passengers and shut down the incoming elevators and escalators. Lily is responsible for explaining these measures to the passengers on the platform.

Dialogue B   The Incoming Elevators and Escalators Are All Out of Service

Activity 5: Think and answer.

1. What happened in the subway?

_____

2. When will the empty train arrive?

_____

Passenger: Excuse me, what's the matter? The incoming elevators and escalators are all out of service.

Lily: Don't panic. As there are too many people at Xizhi Men station and some passengers need to be evacuated.

Passenger: Can you speak more clearly? How can we leave the station?

Lily: Please be calm. We have arranged an empty train to take you to the next station.

Passenger: Really? When will the train arrive?

Lily: It will arrive in about five minutes. You can transfer to Line 6 or take a bus at the next station—Chegongzhuang.

Passenger: I see.

Lily: We apologize for any inconvenience caused.

Activity 6: Listen again and try to tick the right sentences according to dialogue B.

(   ) 1. Only the escalator is closed now.

(   ) 2. The staff is evacuating the passengers because the station is crowded.

(   ) 3. Passengers can transfer to Line 6 at the next station—Chegongzhuang.

Activity 7: Work in pairs.

Practice the dialogue with your partner.

Activity 8: Role play.

Dialogue with given words.

Words and Phrases You May Use

close   crowd   evacuate   calm   transfer

Words and Phrases

explain	[ɪk'spleɪn]	vt.	说明，解释	evacuate	[ɪ'vækjueɪt]	vt.	疏散
inconvenience	[ˌɪnkən'viːniəns]	n.	不便				

Knowledge Expansion

1. Please be ready to exit as the platform is very busy.
   换乘车站乘客较多，请提前做好下车准备。
2. Please queue for entering the subway station.
   请排队进入地铁站。
3. Watch out the rushing crowd.
   请注意拥挤的人群。
4. For safety reasons, we need to evacuate passengers on the platform.
   为安全起见，我们需要疏散站台上的乘客。
5. Please move along the platform to the middle of the train for easier boarding. Thank you.
   请到站台中间位置等候，那里比较容易上车。谢谢！
6. It will be in a short delay because the train is still in the next station. Please accept our apologies!
   由于前方车站的列车还未开出，本次列车的运行将受到延误，敬请谅解。
7. The empty train will arrive in 5 minutes.
   这列空车会在5分钟后到达。
8. If it is busy in this line, you may choose another line for transfer.
   如果您所在的线路乘客较多，您可以选择另一条线来换乘。
9. By the way, how can I leave the platform after I get off the train?
   顺便问一下，我下车后怎么离开站台？
10. That's very easy. The exit is always open.
    那很容易，出口一直可以正常通行。

Exercise 1

Choose Proper Words to Fill in the Blanks

1. Please be _____. (come/calm)
2. You may choose another line for _____. (turn/transfer)
3. We have arranged an _____ train to take you to the next station. (open/empty)
4. Please move along the platform to the middle of the _____ for easier boarding. (concourse/train)

5. Can you _____ more clearly? (ask/speak)

6. Some passengers need to be _____. (evacuated/evacuate)

7. Please follow the _____ on the radio and leave the station in an orderly manner. (instruction/ instructions)

8. We apologize for any _____ (convenience/inconvenience) caused.

9. When _____ the train arrive? (will/may)

Exercise 2

Translate the Following Sentences into English

1. 扶梯停运，楼梯也不能通行了。
2. 您可以换乘6号线或在下一站乘坐公交车。
3. 为了乘客的安全，我们需要关闭这一站。
4. 我下车后怎么离开站台？
5. 我们安排了一列空车将您送到下一站。
6. 我们需要疏散部分乘客。
7. 对给您带来的不便深表歉意。
8. 请提前做好下车准备。
9. 你能说得更清楚一点吗？
10. 请注意拥挤的人群。

Reading and Writing

High Passenger Flow Challenges Beijing Subway's Capacity and Safety

Beijing subway is a rapid transit rail network with 27 lines by the end of 2023. Every day, it takes hundreds of passengers to work or travel. The peak period of Beijing subway starts early in the morning. You can see the ridiculous process of people fighting their way off the train as a horde barely waits to fight their way out, and then the train can hardly get moving  because of all the people crammed in and blocking doors, which is helped by subway officers who shove the last people onto the train. It happens every day in the subway.

High passenger flow challenges Beijing subway's capacity and safety.

In order to ensure the safety of subway operation and to provide better service for passengers, the subway company has taken a series of measures.

First, adjusting the train diagram. As the result, the Batong Line train interval at evening peak is shortened from 3 minutes to 30 seconds. Second, making perfect passenger organization plans, setting up fences in the transfer stations, organizing leading force in the key positions of key stations, as well as through the station broadcasting and slogan guiding passengers to take the escalators in order. Third, organizing volunteers to guide passengers to take the subway orderly. They ensure the station is in order. What's more, strengthening the maintenance quality of vehicles and equipments. Considering the large flow at some lines or transfer stations, Beijing subway also takes temporary measures to limit the passenger flow especially at the morning and evening peak, to make sure the safety of passengers as well as the subway operation.

Words and Phrases

ridiculous	[rɪˈdɪkjələs]	adj.	荒谬的	horde	[hɔːd]	n.	一大群
crammed	[kræmd]	adj.	塞满的；挤满的	capacity	[kəˈpæsəti]	n.	容量；容积
operation	[ˌɒpəˈreɪʃ(ə)n]	n.	操作；运转	interval	[ˈɪntəv(ə)l]	n.	间隔
diagram	[ˈdaɪəɡræm]	n.	图表	as well as			也；还；并且
fence	[fens]	n.	围栏	limit	[ˈlɪmɪt]	vt.	限制；限定
vehicle	[ˈviːəkl]	n.	车辆	especially	[ɪˈspeʃəli]	adv.	特别；尤其
adjust	[əˈdʒʌst]	vt.	调整				

Activity 9: Read and answer.

1. How many measures does Beijing subway take to handle the high passenger flow?
   _____
   _____

2. Can the train interval of the Batong Line at evening peak be shortened according to the measures?

   _____

3. Should the passenger flow be limited during the peak time?
   _____

Activity 10: Read and write (Read the following paragraphs and fill in the blanks with proper words).

transfer	occasions	process	fighting	relieve
shove	network	hardly	fail	onto

Beijing Subway's Rush Hour

What you are looking at is Beijing Subway's Line 13 in the morning, Thursday, July 18th, around 7:30. Xi'erqi station is a _____ station.

It has, like other stations in Beijing's vast transportation _____, built in artificial bottlenecks intended to _____ congestion in the form of gates and narrow staircases. On some _____, however, those _____.

You can see the ridiculous _____ of people _____ their way off the train as a horde barely waits to fight their way out, and then the train can _____ get moving because of all the people crammed in and blocking doors, which is helped by subway attendants (in yellow) who _____ the last people _____ the train.

Communicative Activity

Discuss the following topics in groups of five.

Topic 1: The platform is full, you and your subway colleagues remind passengers to stand outside the yellow line in an orderly manner.

Topic 2: The subway on Line 6 is delayed and passengers need to be evacuated to the next station.

Self-Check

I can speak and write:

☐ transfer	☐ crowd	☐ need to	☐ exceed
☐ inconvenience	☐ explain	☐ follow	☐ flow
☐ capacity	☐ operation	☐ adjust	☐ evacuate

Chapter 11 Cope with High Passenger Flows

I can translate these sentences into Chinese:

☐ 1. You'd better change to another line or take a bus.
☐ 2. For the safety of passengers, we need to close the station.
☐ 3. The exit is always open.
☐ 4. Please follow the instructions on the radio and leave the station in an orderly manner.
☐ 5. We apologize for any inconvenience caused.
☐ 6. Some passengers need to be evacuated.
☐ 7. We have arranged an empty train to take you to the next station.
☐ 8. Watch out the rushing crowd.
☐ 9. If it is busy in this line, you may choose another line for transfer.

I can:

☐ maintain order during peak flow periods.
☐ correctly assess the situation and make decisions when facing high passenger flow.

Complementary Reading

Managing High Passenger Flow in the Subway

Dealing with high passenger flow is a common challenge in subway systems, especially during peak hours or special events. Here are some strategies to cope with a large influx of passengers in the subway:

(1) Increase frequency and capacity: During periods of high demand, consider increasing the frequency of trains and the carrying capacity of each train, which can help accommodate more passengers and reduce overcrowding.

(2) Provide clear information: Display real-time train schedules and announcements about any delays or disruptions at prominent locations within the subway station. Ensure that the information is easily visible and understandable by all passengers. This will help manage expectations and reduce confusion.

(3) Optimize queuing systems: Implement effective queuing systems both inside the station and on platforms to ensure an orderly flow of passengers. Use floor markers or barriers to guide passengers and prevent congestion. Train station staff should be deployed strategically to assist with crowd control if necessary.

(4) Encourage staggered travel times: Promote initiatives that encourage passengers to travel during off-peak hours. This can help distribute passenger flow more evenly throughout the day and alleviate overcrowding during rush hours.

(5) Enhance communication: Train and station staff should be readily available and approachable to answer questions and provide assistance to passengers. Clear signage and

announcements in multiple languages can also enhance communication and ensure that everyone understands important instructions or updates.

(6) Utilize technology: Explore the use of technology to improve the passenger experience. For instance, develop mobile applications or digital platforms that provide real-time information on train availability, crowd levels, and alternative routes. This can empower passengers to make informed decisions and navigate the system more effectively.

(7) Train staff for emergency situations: In the event of an emergency or unexpected situation, ensure that subway employees are well-trained and equipped to handle large crowds safely and efficiently. Conduct regular drills and simulations to familiarize staff with emergency protocols.

(8) Collaborate with other stakeholders: Work closely with relevant authorities, such as local transportation departments, law enforcement agencies, and event organizers to coordinate crowd management efforts effectively. Sharing information and resources can help optimize passenger flow and ensure a smooth subway operation.

Remember that the safety and comfort of passengers are paramount. By implementing these strategies and maintaining open lines of communication, subway operators can better manage high passenger flow and provide a positive travel experience for all commuters.

城市轨道交通客运服务英语
（第3版）

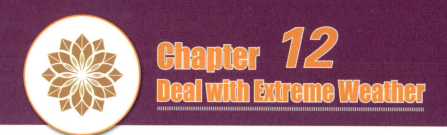

Chapter 12
Deal with Extreme Weather

Objectives

1. Knowledge: Learn the vocabularies and sentences for dealing with extreme weather.
2. Ability: Be able to quickly deal with extreme weather in the subway.
3. Morality: Be adroit and helpful.In the face of unexpected situations, be fearless and fulfill your mission.

Suggested Class Hours

4 class hours

Warm-up

Look at the following pictures and talk about how extreme weather affects the subway.

Listening and Speaking

Scene: Lily provides assistance to the passengers who are worried about the weather.

Dialogue A I Feel Relieved upon Hearing This

Activity 1: Listen and guess.

1. What's the weather like outside the subway station?
   _____
2. Has the water at the entrance and exit been cleaned up?
   _____

Passenger A: It's been raining for almost two hours now.
Passenger B: Yes, I hope the rain will stop when I leave the station because I didn't bring an umbrella with me.
Lily: Don't worry. We have prepared some umbrellas for passengers to borrow at the customer service center.
Passenger A: Really? You are too thoughtful.
Passenger B: The weather is too bad, and the ground at both the entrance and exit is covered with water. We need to be careful not to slip.
Lily: That's right. The subway staff have cleaned up all the water in these areas.
Passenger B: Well, I feel relieved upon hearing this. It's very kind of you.
Lily: It's my pleasure.

Activity 2: Listen again and try to fill in the blanks.

1. We have _____ some _____ for passengers to borrow at the customer service center.
2. I feel _____ upon hearing this.

Activity 3: Work in pairs.
Practice the dialogue with your partner.

Activity 4: Role play.
Dialogue with given words.

Words and Phrases You May Use

rain   umbrella   prepare   area   entrance   exit   slip   pleasure

Words and Phrases

relieve	[rɪ'liːv]	vt.	减轻	clean up			清理干净
careful	['keəf(ə)l]	adj.	小心的	thoughtful	['θɔːtf(ə)l]	adj.	周到；细致
customer service center			客服中心				

Scene: On a snowy day, Wang Dong is evacuating passengers from Dongzhi Men station on Line 2 and reminding them not to slip.

Dialogue B   Thank You for Your Reminder

Activity 5: Think and answer.

1. Why is the Dongzhi Men station on Line 2 closed?
_____

2. What's the weather like today?
_____

Wang Dong: Attention, please! Due to the heavy snow, the Dongzhi Men station on Line 2 will be closed. Please proceed to the nearest exit according to the instructions.

Passenger A: What should I do? I'm gonna be late for work.

Wang Dong: I'm sorry. Please choose another transportation as soon as possible to avoid being late. For safety reasons, please pay attention to slippery floors and walk on non-slip mats.

Passenger A: Thank you for your reminder.

Wang Dong: You're welcome.

Activity 6: Listen again and try to fill in the blanks.

1. Please pay attention to _____ floors and walk on _____ mats.
2. Thank you for your _____ .

Activity 7: Work in pairs.

Practice the dialogue with your partner.

Activity 8: Role play.

Dialogue with given words.

Words and Phrases You May Use

walk on   slippery   floor   reminder

Words and Phrases

| slippery | ['slɪpəri] | adj. | 湿滑的 | non-slip mat | 防滑垫 |
| reminder | [rɪ'maɪndə(r)] | n. | 提示；提醒物 | | |

Knowledge Expansion

1. No Reversing.
   请勿逆行。

2. Please help us to keep the subway litter free.
   请协助我们保持地铁清洁。

107

3. Please proceed to the nearest exit according to the instructions.
   请按照指示前往最近的出口。
4. Please hold the handrail (to balance).
   请抓紧（站稳）扶好。
5. Don't climb on the lift truck.
   严禁攀登升降车。
6. The entrance is temporarily closed.
   此口临时关闭。
7. Don't block access.
   通道禁止停留。
8. Caution! Slippery./Caution! Wet Floor.
   小心地滑。
9. Under construction (repair). Sorry for the inconvenience.
   施工（检修）给您带来不便，请谅解。

Exercise 1

Choose Proper Words to Fill in the Blanks

1. We have prepared some umbrellas for passengers to borrow at the _____ service center.(customer/customers)
2. We need to be _____ not to slip.(carefully/careful)
3. Really? You are too _____.(thoughtful/thoughtfully)
4. The ground at _____ the entrance and exit is covered with water.(both/all)
5. The subway staff have _____ up all the water in these areas.(cleaned/clean)
6. I feel _____ upon hearing this.(relief/relieved)
7. Pay attention to _____ floors and walk on non-slip mats.(slippery/slip)
8. _____ is the weather like outside the subway station?(What/How)
9. The weather is too _____.(bad/badly)
10. Thank you for your _____.(remind/reminder)

Exercise 2

Translate the Following Sentences into English

1. 我们在客服中心准备了一些雨伞供乘客借用。
2. 地铁工作人员已经把这些区域的水都清理干净了。
3. 我很荣幸。
4. 小心地滑！

5. 注意地面湿滑，请走防滑垫。

6. 通道禁止停留。

7. 请勿逆行。

8. 请协助我们保持地铁清洁。

9. 感谢您的提醒。

10. 听到这些话我就放心了。

Reading and Writing

Metro Service During Extreme Weather

Many people rely on the subway to get where they need to go, regardless of the weather. This is why we do everything possible to provide safe and reliable transit service during inclement winter weather.

In many countries, the subway has many pieces of snow equipment available to tackle snow and ice accumulation at stations, rail yards, parking garages, and bus facilities. Hundreds of employees and contractors can be called on to confront snow conditions. During periods of bad weather, the subway may limit or curtail service for safety reasons. There are two facilities usually used in those terrible weathers.

The first facility is called Metrorail. It can be operated very close to a common schedule in snowfall of up to six inches. However, once snow reaches a height of about eight inches, it may be necessary to suspend service above ground. Underground-only operation allows for continuous connections to key activity centers, and helps ensure a more rapid return of full service by protecting train from weather-related damage and allowing crews to focus on clearing snow from above-ground tracks.

The second facility during inclement weather is the Metrobus. Metrobus will reduce service firstly, then limit service to snow emergency routes. If snow accumulates to unsafe levels or road conditions are impassable, subway will halt all bus service until it is safe to resume service. Metrobus has worked with local government to identify snow emergency routes that need to be plowed to maintain bus service to as many communities as possible.

Words and Phrases

extreme	[ɪk'striːm]	adj.	极端的	rely on			依靠
inclement	[ɪn'klemənt]	adj.	气候严酷的；寒冷的	regardless of			不管；不顾
available	[ə'veɪləb(ə)l]	adj.	可利用的	tackle	['tæk(ə)l]	vt.	处理；对付
accumulation	[ə,kjuːmjə'leɪʃn]	n.	积聚；累积	garage	['gæraːʒ]	n.	车库
contractor	[kən'træktə(r)]	n.	承包商	curtail	[kɜː'teɪl]	vt.	缩减
schedule	['ʃedjuːl]	n.	时间表；日程	impassable	[ɪm'paːsəb(ə)l]	adj.	不能通行的
halt	[hɔːlt]	vt.	停止；中止	resume	[rɪ'zjuːm]	vt.	重新开始
route	[ruːt]	n.	路线	plow	[plaʊ]	vt.	用铲雪机铲雪
identify	[aɪ'dentɪfaɪ]	vt.	鉴定；识别	community	[kə'mjuːnəti]	n.	社区，社会

Activity 9: Read and answer.

1. How many pieces of snow equipment are there for the subway?

   _____

2. What does the subway do during periods of terrible weather?

   _____

3. What can the Metrorail do in the snowfall?

   _____

Activity 10: Read and write (Read the following paragraphs and fill in the blanks with proper words).

forecast	notice	ready	schedule	alert
expect	freezing	tunnels	temperature	created

Winter Subway Service in Beijing

Due to (由于) the _____ of a brutal (无情的) winter storm beginning this evening, some Beijing subway lines will not operate normally or according to the printed _____. To help _____ passengers, the subway company has _____ an informative poster (告示) to _____ riders of what to _____.

Heavy snow, ice and _____ rain require that the out-of-service trains are stored in subway _____ rather than left in outside yards. This insures that trains will be _____ for tomorrow morning's rush hour service and the car interior (内部) will maintain a comfortable (舒适的) _____.

Communicative Activity

Discuss the following topics in groups of five.

Topic 1: There is a storm outside the station, and many people rush into the subway station. The crowd is dense, and the ground is covered with water. Lily serves the passengers at the station.

Topic 2: Due to excessive foot traffic, the Xizhi Men station on Line 2 will be closed. The station entrance is damp due to the heavy snow outside. Wang Dong is serving passengers by the stairs.

Self-Check

I can speak and write:

☐ prepare   ☐ customer service center   ☐ rely on   ☐ impassable
☐ slippery   ☐ floor   ☐ umbrella   ☐ relieve
☐ instruction   ☐ inclement   ☐ caution   ☐ non-slip mat
☐ extreme   ☐ tackle   ☐ curtail

I can translate these sentences into Chinese:

☐ 1. We have prepared some umbrellas for passengers to borrow at the customer service center.

Chapter 12 Deal with Extreme Weather

111

☐2. The weather is too bad, and the ground at both the entrance and exit is covered with water. We need to be careful not to slip.

☐3. Really? You're too thoughtful.

☐4. The subway staff have cleaned up all the water in these areas.

☐5. Please proceed to the nearest exit according to the instructions.

☐6. Due to the heavy snow, the Dongzhi Men station on Line 2 will be closed.

☐7. Well, I feel relieved upon hearing this.

☐8. Please pay attention to slippery floors and walk on non-slip mats.

I can:

☐ provide service to passengers in extreme weather conditions.

☐ handle problems that may occur at subway stations in extreme weather.

Complementary Reading

Chongqing Subway Stations Provide Rest Areas in Summer

To help people escape from summer heat, Chongqing urban rail transit operator set up rest areas in 113 stations across the city on Wednesday.

At the air-conditioned stations, a designated rest area is equipped with chairs, drink dispensers(饮水机) and a first-aid box. Anyone wanting to cool off can take a seat inside for free.

This facility is especially welcomed by the seniors and outdoor workers.

The residents of Chongqing, southwest China are experiencing unusually hot weather this summer. Forecasts show temperatures as high as 40 degrees Celsius in several parts of the city in coming days, making such facilities even more popular.

(Photo provided by China Daily.com.cn)

(https://global.chinadaily.com.cn/a/202307/13/WS64afa6f3a31035260b81640f_2.html)

Chapter 13
Cope with Emergencies

Objectives

1. Knowledge: Learn the vocabularies and sentences for coping with emergencies.
2. Ability: Can deal with emergent accidents quickly.
3. Morality: In the face of emergent accidents, be calm and fearless.

Suggested Class Hours

4 class hours

Warm-up

Learn the application scenarios of subway warning signs. Talk to your classmates about your understanding of subway emergencies.

A — Caution, Gap

B — Caution, Risk of Pinching Hand

C — Leaning on the Door Prohibited

D — EMERGENCY EXITS AT ENDS OF TRAIN

E — EMERGENCY CALL (EMERGENCY USE ONLY)

F — Open the door in emergency only. Turn the handle along the unlocking direction. Open the door after the train stops. Dangerous! No mishandling!

Listening and Speaking

Scene: The fire alarm on the plat form sounded, and Wang Dong is evacuating passengers.

Dialogue A   What's the Matter?

Activity 1: Listen and guess.

1. Why did the fire alarm on the plat form sound?
_____
2. Where do the passengers exit the station?
_____

Passenger: What's the matter? Why did the fire alarm on the platform sound?
Wang Dong: A carriage in the station caught fire.
Passenger: Ah. So what should we do?
Wang Dong: Don't worry. The fire has been extinguished. Please follow the instructions on the subway broadcast to exit the station in an orderly manner.
Passenger: Where do we exit the station?
Wang Dong: Please follow the evacuation signs to exit from the middle platform.
Passenger: Thank you.
Wang Dong: You are welcome.

Activity 2: Listen again and try to fill in the blanks.

1. What's the _____?
2. Don't _____. The fire has been _____. Please _____ the instructions on the subway _____ to exit the station.

Activity 3: Work in pairs.
Practice the dialogue with your partner.

Activity 4: Role play.
Dialogue with given words.

Words and Phrases You May Use

matter   extinguish   alarm   follow the instructions   welcome

Words and Phrases

matter	['mætə(r)]	n. 原因；事件	follow	['fɒləʊ]	vt. 跟随；遵循
instruction	[ɪn'strʌkʃ(ə)n]	n. 指导	evacuation	[ɪˌvækjuː'eɪʃ(ə)n]	n. 疏散；撤离
sign	[saɪn]	n. 指示；标记			

Scene: A newly arrived train has experienced a power outage, and the carriage is pitch black. Lily is guiding the passengers.

Dialogue B   All the Lights Have Gone out

Activity 5: Think and answer.

1. What happened in the train carriage?

_____

2. Can the passengers wait for the next train at the station?

_____

Passenger: What is going on? All the lights have gone out.
Lily: Don't worry. I'll ask the station management office.
Passenger: What should we do?
Lily: Please be patient and wait for a moment.
(After a while, the doors of the train open. Then the broadcast said, "Attention please. There's an emergency on the train. Please get off the train in an orderly manner.")
Lily: Everyone get off the train according to the instructions and guidance of the staff.
Passenger: Can I wait here for the next train?
Lily: No, we have to leave the station now. We apologize for any inconvenience caused to you.

Activity 6: Listen again and try to fill in the blanks.

1. Everyone get off the train according to the _____ and _____ of the staff.
2. All the lights have _____ .

Activity 7: Work in pairs.

Practice the dialogue with your partner.

Activity 8: Role play.

Dialogue with given words.

Words and Phrases You May Use

be patient   wait for   get off

Words and Phrases

power outage			停电	moment	['məʊmənt]	n.	片刻
carriage	['kærɪdʒ]	n.	车厢	emergency	[ɪ'mɜːdʒənsi]	n.	紧急情况
patient	['peɪʃ(ə)nt]	adj.	有耐心的	wait for			等待
pitch black			漆黑一片	guide	[gaɪd]	vt.	指导

115

Knowledge Expansion

1. We are now closing the station for your safety. Thank you for your understanding.
   为了您的安全，现在关闭车站。感谢您的理解。
2. Don't lean on the doors.
   请勿倚靠车门。
3. Be careful! It's dangerous!
   小心！危险！
4. All passengers, please be careful and stay back.
   各位乘客，请注意安全，保持距离。
5. Please stand behind the yellow line while waiting for the train.
   请您站在安全候车线以内候车。
6. Don't be crowded, please.
   请勿拥挤。
7. Never chase or play in the station or on the train.
   严禁在站内、车厢内追逐、打闹。
8. Watch out for the door.
   请小心车门。
9. Please follow the instructions of the station staff and leave the station in an orderly manner.
   请按车站工作人员的指引有序地离开车站。

Exercise 1

Choose Proper Words to Fill in the Blanks

1. What's the _____? (matter/up)
2. Please follow the _____ of the station staff and leave the station in an orderly manner. (instructions/instruct)
3. Everyone get _____ the train according to the instructions and guidance of the staff.(off/out)
4. Please follow the evacuation signs to exit from the middle _____. (road/platform)
5. What _____ we do? (are/should)
6. Please be _____ and wait for a moment. (patient/patience)
7. I'll _____ the station management office. (ask/asked)
8. Can I wait here _____ the next train? (for/of)
9. We have to _____ the station now. (go/leave)
10. Don't be _____, please.(crowd/crowded)

Exercise 2

Translate the Following Sentences into English

1. 我们该怎么办？
2. 本次列车出现了突发情况，请有序下车。

3.请勿倚靠车门。
4.小心！危险。
5.请跟随疏散标志从站台中部出站。
6.别担心，火已经熄灭了。
7.站内的一个车厢着火了。
8.请勿拥挤。
9.各位乘客，请注意安全，保持距离。
10.严禁在站内、车厢内追逐、打闹。

Reading and Writing

Subway Escalator Accidents Call for Security Guarantee

Although the development of subway transit has brought a great deal of convenience to passengers, accidents in recent years have led to calls for strengthening security and maintenance.

Recently a dozen escalators on the capital city's YIZHUANG Line have been recalled, because they have the same risk of malfunction as the one that took the life of a 13-year-old boy on July 5th. The accident happened around 9:30 a.m. at the exit of the Beijing Zoo station on Subway Line 4. The municipal government's information office said some people on the escalator fell down after an escalator malfunction.

Beijing MTR Corporation, operator of the line, posted a brief statement about the accident on its website. The company said it had already launched an emergency response and all injured people had been sent to the hospital. A probe had begun over the cause of the accident.

"Subway companies should raise standards concerning escalator purchases and choose more sturdy products according to the requirements of Chinese subway system. The buyers should be self-critical, rather than always point fingers at escalator manufacturers whenever accidents occur." an e-mail said.

Words and Phrases

statement	['steɪtmənt]	n.	声明	maintenance	['meɪntənəns]	n. 维护
launch	[lɔːnʃ]	vt.	发动，发起	probe	[prəʊb]	n. 调查
sturdy	['stɜːdi]	adj.	坚固的	purchase	['pɜːtʃəs]	n. 购买
manufacturer	[ˌmænjuˈfæktʃərə(r)]	n.	制造商	brief	[briːf]	adj. 简短的
recent	['riːs(ə)nt]	adj.	最近的			

Activity 9: Read and answer.

1. What is the reason for the mentioned escalator accident?
   _____

2. Do you know why the maintenance of subway is poor?
   _____

Activity 10: Read and write (Read the following paragraphs and fill in the blanks with proper words).

| fully open | on time | cross | get on | on average |
| according to | safety | before | platform | staff |

Obey the Subway Rules for the Sake of our Safety

We must obey the subway rules for the sake of our safety. Here are some rules of which we should remind (提醒) all the passengers:

(1) When moving to the _____ through turnstile (十字转门) with ticket, if any malfunction occurs when using the ticket, don't pat or smash (拍击) the machine. You should ask the _____ for help.

(2) You should not _____ over the safety line (the yellow line) on the ground when you are waiting for the train.

(3) When the train's doors and the screen doors are _____, the passengers should _____ the train after those who are getting off the train.

(4) The signal light above every train's door will twinkle (闪亮) _____ the train starts moving. There will be regular beeps (鸣叫) when the door is closing, by this time, those who haven't got on the train yet should not cross the _____ line.

(5) The intervals (间隔) between trains are different, the sooner the train can depart

from the station, the better the following train can get into the station _____. The train is so crowded that passengers cannot get on, don't grab (紧抓) the door but assist (协助) the staff to let the train depart on time.

(6) The time each train stays in the station is different _____ the ridership (客流量), which is 30 to 40 seconds _____, so please get fully prepared before you get off the train.

Communicative Activity

Discuss the following topics in groups of five.

Topic 1: A woman fell on the platform and crowd screamed. The subway staff is helping the woman up and maintaining passenger order.

Topic 2: A fire broke out at the station, and subway staff is guiding the passengers to evacuate the station.

Self-Check

I can speak and write:

☐ matter ☐ guide ☐ extinguish ☐ follow
☐ recent ☐ probe ☐ sturdy ☐ according to
☐ evacuation ☐ brief ☐ patient ☐ purchase
☐ power outage ☐ emergency ☐ moment

I can translate these sentences into Chinese:

☐ 1. What's the matter?
☐ 2. What should we do?
☐ 3. Don't be crowded, please.
☐ 4. Please follow the evacuation signs to exit from the middle platform.
☐ 5. Please follow the instructions on the subway broadcast to exit the station in an orderly manner.
☐ 6. Please be patient and wait for a moment.
☐ 7. Don't worry. I'll ask the station management office.
☐ 8. Don't lean on the doors.
☐ 9. Be careful! It's dangerous!
☐ 10. All passengers, please be careful and stay back.

I can:

☐ maintain passenger order in emergency situations.

☐provide assistance to passengers in times of emergency.

Complementary Reading

"Eyes on the Real World": Beijing Subway Adds Warnings for Phone Addicts

New warning signs urging passengers to stop being glued to their smart phones have recently been found their way onto multiple lines of the Beijing subway.

The signs feature the famous no-smoking style red circle with a line through it, on top of a figure arched over their mobile phone, complete with the words "Eyes on the Real World" written in English and Chinese. Posted throughout stations, on escalators and inside the subway carriages themselves, the signs are designed to remind passengers of the dangers of being distracted by their smartphones while taking public transportation.

(Source(s): CGTN)
(https://news.cgtn.com/news/3d59444d774d6a4d/index.html?t=1486624946531)

Chapter 14
Passenger First Aid

Objectives

1. Knowledge: Learn the vocabularies and sentences of passenger first aid.
2. Ability: Be able to provide first aid to passengers.
3. Morality: Have a kind heart and be enthusiastic about helping others.

Suggested Class Hours

4 class hours

Warm-up

What are the diseases that passengers who need first aid usually suffer from in the subway? Can you talk to your classmates about the sudden illnesses that people may get?

Listening and Speaking

Scene: A passenger on the platform suddenly fell chest pain, and Lily approached to inquire.

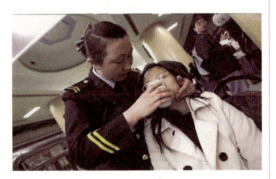

Dialogue A Do You Feel Better Now?

Activity 1: Listen and guess.

1. What's wrong with the passenger?
_____
2. Does the passenger have any medicine with her?
_____

Lily: Hello. My name is Lily. You look very painful. Can I help you?
Passenger: I have chest pain, dizziness, and difficult breathing.
Lily: Do you need me to call an ambulance for you?
Passenger: Yes, thank you.
Lily: Do you have any medicine with you?
Passenger: Yes. It's in my right pocket.
Lily: OK. I found it. I will get you a glass of water.
(Lily brought a glass of water to the passenger. A moment later…)
Lily: Do you feel better now?
Passenger: Yes. I feel much better. Thank you for your help.
Lily: My pleasure. I'll take you to the customer service center to rest.
Passenger: Thank you very much.

Activity 2: Listen again and try to fill in the blanks.

1. You look very _____.
2. Do you have any _____ with you?

Activity 3: Work in pairs.

Practice the dialogue with your partner.

Activity 4: Role play.

Dialogue with given words.

Words and Phrases You May Use

dizziness   medicine   help   ambulance   chest pain

Words and Phrases

pain	[peɪn]	n.	疼痛	feel better		感觉好点
chest	[tʃest]	n.	胸	my pleasure		不客气；乐意效劳
dizziness	[ˈdɪzinəs]	n.	头晕	a glass of		一杯
breathe	[briːð]	vi.	呼吸	ambulance	[ˈæmbjələns]	n. 救护车

Scene: A passenger fainted at the subway station, and his companion shouted for help. Wang Dong rushed up to help him.

Dialogue B Time Is Life

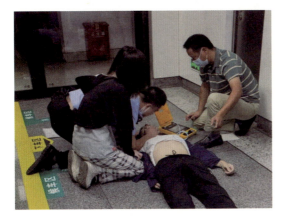
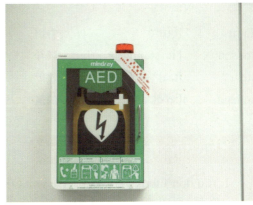

Activity 5: Think and answer.

1. What's wrong with the passenger?

_____

2. Do they call an ambulance?

_____

Passenger: Help! Please!

Wang Dong: Don't worry. What's wrong with him?

Passenger: Oh, he fainted. Please help him.

Wang Dong: Calm down. I'll call an ambulance.

Passenger: Troubling you. Thank you.

Wang Dong: OK. The ambulance will arrive soon. Let him lie down and loose his tie.

Passenger: Thank you very much indeed.

Wang Dong: Time is life. Let me check his pulse and do CPR quickly.

Passenger: I really appreciate it.

Wang Dong: It's my pleasure.

Activity 6: Listen again and try to fill in the blanks.

1. Oh, he _____. Please _____ him.

2. I'll call an _____.

Activity 7: Work in pairs.

Practice the dialogue with your partner.

Activity 8: Role play.

Dialogue with given words.

Words and Phrases You May Use

help   faint   check for   CPR   pulse

Chapter 14 Passenger First Aid

Words and Phrases

faint	[feɪnt]	vi.	昏倒	pulse	[pʌls]		n.	脉搏
loosen	['luːs(ə)n]	vt.	解开	calm down				冷静
tie	[taɪ]	n.	领带	companion	[kəm'pænjən]		n.	同伴
indeed	[ɪn'diːd]	adv.	的确					

Knowledge Expansion

1. You don't look very well. Are you OK?
   你看上去生病了，没事吧？
2. Do you need a doctor?
   您需要请医生吗？
3. Please sit down for a rest.
   请坐下来休息一下吧。
4. It seems like you're having a heart attack.
   您好像是心脏病发作了。
5. Do you have any medicine with you?
   您身上带着药吗？
6. Do you feel better now?
   您现在觉得好些了吗？
7. Shall I call an ambulance for you?
   需要我为您叫一辆救护车吗？
8. Let's see what I can do to relieve your pain.
   我们看看如何能减轻你的疼痛。
9. Shall I inform your family or friends?
   需要我通知您的家人或朋友吗？
10. I'll be fine after taking some medicine.
    吃了药我就会好了。

Exercise 1

Choose Proper Words to Fill in the Blanks

1. I'll _____ you to the customer service center to rest. (take/make)
2. You look very _____. (pain/painful)
3. I will _____ you a glass of water. (get/make)
4. I have chest pain, dizziness, and difficult _____. (breathe/breathing)
5. Do you have any medicine _____ you? (with/in)

6. You don't look very _____. (good/well)
7. _____ is life. (Time/Times)
8. Shall I _____ your family or friends? (inform/informing)
9. Shall I _____ an ambulance for you? (ask/call)
10. I'll be fine after _____ some medicine. (take/taking)

Exercise 2

Translate the Following Sentences into English

1. 你看上去生病了，没事吧？
2. 我来叫一辆救护车吧。
3. 请坐下来休息一下吧。
4. 您现在觉得好些了吗？
5. 需要我为您叫一辆救护车吗？
6. 让他躺下，解开他的领带。
7. 时间就是生命。
8. 让我检查一下他的脉搏，然后快速进行心肺复苏。
9. 您好像是心脏病发作了。
10. 需要我通知您的家人或朋友吗？

Reading and Writing

Passengers Gave First Aid to a Female Fainting in the Subway

It is reported that three passengers worked together to give first aid to a woman who fainted at the People's Square Station on Thursday morning, and a few subway commuters stepped up to offer help.

According to a witness, a male doctor put on a pair of medical gloves, bolstered the fainted woman's head up with her bag and did some checking.

A moment later, another female, who was a Traditional Chinese Medicine doctor, also joined the rescue. According to the witness, they gave a simple massage to the woman to help her wake up when station officers and an ambulance were called.

The sick woman returned to consciousness when the ambulance arrived. She refused to be sent to the hospital, saying she was feeling all right, and left the station on her own. The station officer said the three passengers did not leave any contact information after the incident.

Words and Phrases

commuter	[kəˈmjuːtə(r)]	n.	通勤的人	bolster	[ˈbəʊlstə(r)]	vt.	支撑
massage	[ˈmæsɑːʒ]	n.	按摩	female	[ˈfiːmeɪl]	n.	女子
witness	[ˈwɪtnəs]	n.	目击者	consciousness	[ˈkɒnʃəsnəs]	n.	知觉
refuse	[rɪˈfjuːz]	vt.	拒绝	incident	[ˈɪnsɪdənt]	n.	事故
on one's own			独自	traditional	[trəˈdɪʃən(ə)l]	adj.	传统的
step up			走上前	wake up			苏醒
according to			根据				

Activity 9: Read and answer.

1. Which subway station did the woman faint at?
_____
2. How did the male doctor help the fainted woman?
_____
3. How did the Traditional Chinese Medicine doctor rescue the fainted woman?
_____
4. Did the passengers leave their contact information after the incident?
_____

Activity 10: Read and write (Read the following paragraphs and fill in the blanks with proper words).

| lost | arrived | subway | duty | aid |
| call | hour | to | passengers | professional |

First Aid Training for Subway Staff to Give Help Fast

The first team of the city subway's first aid staff will be on _____ after first aid training (培训) in respond _____ emergencies (紧急情况) like passengers fainting on the _____. The subway staff trained in first _____ course will be more _____ and confident (有信心) when doing first aid now.

In the past, the common practice was to _____ the emergency line and escort (陪伴) the patients to an ambulance or rescue workers. That meant the "golden _____" to save a life can be _____ as they waited. Resuscitation (营救) would be made until an ambulance _____.

More qualified (合格的) staff will be introduced (引进) with the growth of the subway network, which handle up to more and more _____.

Communicative Activity

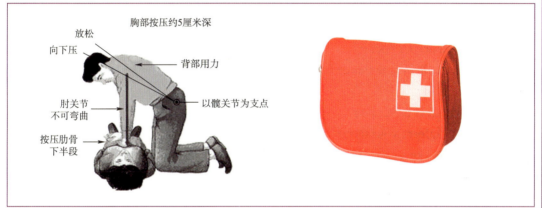

Discuss the following topics in groups of five.

Topic 1: A foreign male passenger suddenly lost consciousness and collapsed in his seat on the subway Line 2 train. As a subway staff, what will you do?

Topic 2: Practice the following first aid steps in your group.

- Danger—Check if the passenger is in danger.
- Response—Check for a response by shouting a command at him and gently shaking his shoulders, then check for severe bleeding and other injuries.
- Airway—Help him to breathe by opening their airways. Do this by placing one hand on the forehead and using two fingers to lift the chin.
- Breathing—Check if he is breathing by looking for his chest moving and listening for his breaths. If he is not breathing, begin resuscitation (CPR).
- Call for help—Call 120 for help.

Self-Check

I can speak and write:

☐ pain ☐ breathe ☐ passenger ☐ heart attack
☐ ambulance ☐ faint ☐ rescue ☐ take medicine
☐ pulse ☐ CPR ☐ first aid ☐ step up
☐ commuter ☐ incident ☐ refuse ☐ witness

I can translate these sentences into Chinese:

☐ 1. You don't look very well. Are you OK?
☐ 2. Do you need a doctor?
☐ 3. Shall I call an ambulance for you?
☐ 4. Time is life.
☐ 5. Do you feel better now?
☐ 6. Shall I inform your family or friends?
☐ 7. It seems like you're having a heart attack.
☐ 8. What's wrong with him?
☐ 9. Please sit down for a rest.

I can:

☐ provide services for uncomfortable passengers.
☐ provide first aid to emergency passengers.

Complementary Reading

Beijing to Equip Subway System with AEDs, Raising First Aid Awareness

Beijing is going to equip all subway stations in the city with first-aid devices automated external defibrillators (AEDs)(自动体外除颤器) by the end of 2022, the municipal transport and health authorities jointly announced on Tuesday.

The installation started on Tuesday and by the end of this year, at least 104 stations  on seven subway lines in the Chinese capital will be equipped with the AEDs. And by 2022, at least 80 percent of the subway staff will be properly trained for using the AEDs, according to Beijing Municipal Commission of Transport and Beijing Municipal Health Commission.

AED is a type of medical device that can analyze heart rhythm and deliver an electrical shock if necessary, to help a person suffering sudden cardiac arrest (心脏骤停)restore effective rhythm. It is easy to use, and therefore is considered one of most effective first-aid devices to be placed in public areas.

(Source(s): CGTN)

(https://news.cgtn.com/news/2020-10-28/Beijing-to-equip-subway-system-with-AEDs-raising-first-aid-awareness-UWajfQRiTK/index.html)

城市轨道交通客运服务英语
（第3版）

Chapter 15
Have a Good Journey

🦅 Objectives

1. Knowledge: Learn the vocabularies and sentences for providing high-quality services.
2. Ability: Can provide high-quality services to passengers.
3. Morality: Help others, enthusiastically and thoughtfully.

🌱 Suggested Class Hours

4 class hours

🌱 Warm-up

With China's fast development, more and more foreigners have come to China for further study or travel. As subway staff, Wang Dong and Lily know they should offer high-quality services to passengers and make great efforts to be _____.

😊 Cheerful   😊 Attentive   😊 Responsible   😊 Empathetic

Listening and Speaking

Scene: Lily is going on a tour of inspection on the platform and sees a foreigner carrying heavy luggage. She steps forward to help the passenger.

Dialogue A　I'm Looking Forward to These Wonderful Culture Journeys

Activity 1: Listen and guess.

1. Why does Lily step forward to help the passenger?

_____

2. What other help does the passenger need from Lily?

_____

Lily: Good morning, sir. Your luggage is quite heavy, may I help you?

Passenger: Thank you, could you help me put it in the waiting area?

Lily: Sure, do you need any other help?

Passenger: I just came to China, can you tell me how to better understand Chinese culture?

Lily: No problem, Beijing subway you are taking is a journey of Chinese culture. Every subway line presents a characteristic of Chinese culture.

Passenger: Wow, it's great.

Lily: You can see the blue and white porcelain decorated in Beitucheng Station on Line 8.

Passenger: Really? I'm looking forward to these wonderful cultural journeys. Thank you so much, goodbye.

Lily: It's my pleasure. Have a nice journey.

Activity 2: Listen again and try to fill in the blanks.

1. Could you help me put it in the _____?
2. It's my _____. Have a nice _____.

Activity 3: Work in pairs.

Practice the dialogue with your partner.

Activity 4: Role play.

Dialogue with given words.

Words and Phrases You May Use

help　　present　　culture　　pleasure　　wonderful

Words and Phrases

waiting area			候车区	blue and white porcelain			青花瓷
journey	['dʒɜːni]	n.	旅程	decorate	['dekəreɪt]	vt.	装饰

Scene: Lily and Wang Dong are discussing their future work prospects in the subway.

Dialogue B I Want to Become an Excellent Subway Staff

Activity 5: Think and answer.

1. What are they discussing?

_____

2. What are their career goals?

_____

Wang Dong: Hi, Lily, how have you been lately?

Lily: Not bad, and you?

Wang Dong: I'm okey too, time flies so fast.

Lily: Yes, this period of time is truly unforgettable. I am excited when I think about my future work in the Beijing subway.

Wang Dong: Yes, me too. I will do my best to provide high-quality services for passengers.

Lily: My thoughts are the same as yours. Wishing you success.

Wang Dong: Let's work together. I think there is still a lot to learn about passenger service.

Lily: Yes, to become an excellent subway staff, one also needs to learn civility and etiquette from different countries.

Wang Dong: Not only that, you also need to show a smile at last.

Lily: I will. Thank you.

Activity 6: Listen again and try to fill in the blanks.

1. I will do my best to provide _____ for passengers.

2. _____ you success.

Activity 7: Work in pairs.

Practice the dialogue with your partner.

Activity 8: Role play.

Dialogue with given words.

Words and Phrases You May Use

excited   thought   service   not only   smile   civility

Words and Phrases

unforgettable	[ˌʌnfə'getəb(ə)l]	adj.	令人难忘的	excellent	['eksələnt]	adj.	优秀的
future	['fjuːtʃə(r)]	n.	未来	etiquette	['etɪkət]	n.	礼仪

Knowledge Expansion

1. Could you help me put it over there, the waiting area?
   您可以帮我把这个放到候车区那儿吗？
2. Wow, that sounds great.
   哇，听起来很不错。
3. It's very kind of you.
   您真是太好了。
4. Have a nice journey.
   祝您旅途愉快。
5. How unforgettable it is!
   多么令人难以忘怀！
6. Wishing you success.
   祝您成功。
7. We still need to strengthen our training for service skills and knowledge.
   我们仍然需要加强服务技能和知识的培训。
8. Civility and etiquette play an important role in our work.
   文明礼仪在我们的工作中起着十分重要的作用。
9. I'm really looking forward to the job in the future.
   我真的非常期待未来的工作。
10. Show your beautiful smile when you are offering a service.
    在你提供服务时，展示你迷人的微笑。

Exercise 1

Choose Proper Words to Fill in the Blanks

1. Could you help me put it _____ the waiting area? (in/into)

2. It's very kind _____ you. (of/to)
3. Can you tell me how to _____ understand Chinese culture? (good/better)
4. Beijing subway you are taking is a _____ of Chinese culture. (journey/journeys)
5. Have _____ nice journey. (a/an)
6. How have you _____ lately? (be/been)
7. I think there is still a lot to learn _____ passenger service. (to/about)
8. Civility and etiquette play _____ important role in our work. (an/a)
9. _____ you success. (Wishing/Wished)

Exercise 2

Translate the Following Sentences into English

1. 你最近怎么样？
2. 文明礼仪在我们的工作中起着十分重要的作用。
3. 祝您成功。
4. 祝您旅途愉快。
5. 多么令人难以忘怀！
6. 我真的非常期待未来的工作。
7. 您真是太好了。
8. 您可以帮我把这个放到候车区那儿吗？
9. 在你提供服务时，展示你迷人的微笑。
10. 我们仍然需要加强服务技能和知识的培训。

Reading and Writing

Subway Could Do More for the Blind

A blind man fell from the platform at the Railway Station of subway Line 4 and onto the tracks last month. He was rescued by two passengers before the train's arrival but he suffered severe internal injuries and had to undergo a surgery.

The reasons of the incident are under investigation. The lack of the protective measures for the blind may be one of the reasons. So all the subway stations should pay more attention to the protective measures and facilities for the blind.

Transferring is more difficult for the blind. It is almost impossible for the blind to transfer from one line to another in subway. In addition, it's hard for them to know what happens especially unexpected malfunction without any signs and announcements in Braille in the subway.

So, the subway company could do more for the blind.

Words and Phrases

| rescue | ['reskjuː] | vt. | 营救 | internal | [ɪn'tɜːn(ə)l] | adj. | 内部的 |
| undergo | [ˌʌndə'gəʊ] | vt. | 经历 | | | | |

Activity 9: Read and answer.

1. What could the subway company do for the blind?
   _____

2. Why should all the subway stations pay more attention to the protective measures and facilities for the blind?
   _____

Activity 10: Read and write (Read the following paragraphs and fill in the blanks with proper words).

| skills | training | commuters | provided | passenger |
| presently | program | seek | services | special |

Subway Trains its Staff in Sign Language for Deaf and Dumb

The subway has started _____ for Customer Relation Assistants in sign language for deaf and dumb people to ensure that such _____, while traveling in the subway are looked after, guided and _____ a comfortable ride.

This training _____ will help the staff in understanding sign language of disabled people

136

who travel in the subway. These persons can _____ assistance (帮助) from the station staff by informing in advance so that they can be provided necessary assistance in time. _____, the subway staff are also given special training in First Aid, Customer Care, Spoken English and Communication _____ at the subway training institute by specialized (专门的) agencies. The subway staff also have the _____ programs in order to offer high-quality _____ for every _____.

Communicative Activity

Discuss the following topics in groups of five.

Topic 1: Xiao Li just arrived in Beijing yesterday and is not familiar with the subway system. Please provide him with assistance.

Topic 2: Claire is an international student who wants to become a volunteer for subway services. What advice can you give her?

Self-Check

I can speak and write:

- ☐ luggage
- ☐ culture
- ☐ etiquette
- ☐ step forward to
- ☐ excellent
- ☐ undergo
- ☐ unforgettable
- ☐ rescue
- ☐ play an important role
- ☐ internal

I can translate these sentences into Chinese:

☐ 1. How have you been lately?
☐ 2. Could you help me put it in the waiting area?

Chapter 15　Have a Good Journey

☐3. Have a nice journey.
☐4. Time flies so fast.
☐5. I will do my best to provide high-quality services for passengers.
☐6. Wishing you success.
☐7. I'm really looking forward to the job in the future.
☐8. Civility and etiquette play an important role in our work.
☐9. That sounds great.

I can:

☐provide high-quality services for passengers.
☐work hard become an excellent subway staff.

Complementary Reading

How to Become an Excellent Subway Employee

Being an outstanding employee is essential when working in the subway system. It requires a strong work ethic, excellent communication skills, and a commitment to providing exceptional services to passengers. Here are some tips on how to become an excellent subway employee:

(1) Knowledge and Skills: A good subway employee should have a thorough understanding of the subway network, including different lines, stations, and fare systems. They should also be knowledgeable about safety procedures and emergency protocols. Continuous learning and update on new developments in the subway system are crucial to provide accurate information and assist passengers effectively.

(2) Customer Service: Providing exceptional customer service is paramount. A friendly and approachable demeanor when dealing with passengers is essential. Be proactive in helping passengers, answering their queries, and assisting with directions. Patience and empathy are key qualities that can make a significant difference in creating a positive experience for passengers.

(3) Communication: Effective communication skills are crucial for subway employees. They should have clear and concise verbal communication to address passenger needs and announce upcoming stops or station information. Additionally, written communication skills are essential for creating signage and informative materials for passengers.

(4) Problem-solving: Quick thinking and problem-solving abilities are vital in handling unexpected situations. Being able to think on your feet and find solutions to challenges will ensure the smooth operation of the subway system. Remain calm and composed during emergencies, help coordinate with relevant authorities, and take appropriate actions to ensure passengers safety.

(5) Teamwork: Collaboration and teamwork are fundamental in a fast-paced environment like the subway system. Coordinate with colleagues, supervisors, and other departments to ensure efficient operations. Assist fellow employees when needed, share knowledge, and contribute to a positive work atmosphere.

(6) Punctuality and Reliability: Being punctual and reliable demonstrates professionalism and dedication. Arriving on time for shifts and adhering to schedules is crucial for keeping the subway system running smoothly. Reliability is essential to gain the trust of supervisors, colleagues, and passengers.

(7) Personal Safety: Always prioritize personal safety and the safety of passengers. Follow all safety protocols and guidelines strictly. Be knowledgeable about evacuation procedures and emergency exits in case of unforeseen events.

Remember, becoming an excellent subway employee is not just about fulfilling your job responsibilities but also about creating a positive and comfortable experience for passengers. By incorporating these qualities into your work ethic, you can contribute to the efficient functioning of the subway system and make a lasting impression on passengers.

References

［1］阎国强，仇海兵. 城市轨道交通概论［M］. 3版. 北京：人民交通出版社股份有限公司，2021.

［2］高蓉. 城市轨道交通客运服务［M］. 3版. 北京：人民交通出版社股份有限公司，2021.

［3］陶曙教，刘伶俐. 轨道交通客运服务实用英语口语[M]. 2版. 北京：中国铁道出版社，2009.

［4］卢小萍. 公交乘务英语100句［M］. 北京：北京语言大学出版社，2004.

［5］赵巍巍. 城市轨道交通客运服务英语［M］. 3版. 北京：人民交通出版社股份有限公司，2020.

［6］李建民. 城市轨道交通专业英语［M］. 2版. 北京：机械工业出版社，2015.

附录1
候车、指路、安全乘车、出站、帮助等常见词汇与服务用语

常见词汇

英文	中文	英文	中文
screen door	屏蔽门	platform	站台
safety line	安全线	follow the instructions	根据指示
go straight	直行	turn left	左转
turn right	右转	five minutes' walk/ five-minute walk	步行5分钟路程
go upstairs	上楼	go downstairs	下楼
first train	头班车	last train	末班车
next train	下次列车	train headway	列车运行间隔时间
peak/rush hours	高峰期	off-peak time	非高峰期
over travel	超程	excess fare	补票
get off/on	下/上车	direct	直达
change/ transfer	换乘	tap in/out	刷卡进/出站

服务用语

英文	中文
Mind the gap.	小心空隙。
Please don't go beyond the yellow safety line.	请不要超越黄色安全线。
Please don't lean on the screen door.	请不要倚靠屏蔽门。
It takes about 10 minutes.	大概需要10分钟。
Please pay the excess fare.	请补票。
Please let the passengers off the train first.	请先下后上。
Where would you like to go?	您想去哪?
Take it easy.	不要着急。
Please stand clear of the door.	请离车门远一点。
Passengers with bulky baggage, please use the elevator.	携带大件行李的乘客,请使用升降电梯。
Please wait for the train at the opposite platform.	请在对面站台候车。
Your ticket is over travel.	您的票超程了。
Please stand firm and hold the handrail.	请站稳扶好。
Please get ready to get off the subway.	请准备下车。

附录2 宣传用语

英文	中文
Please stand outside the yellow line, hold the card in your right hand, swipe the card and get into the station, children first.	请您站在黄线外，右手持卡，刷卡进站，儿童先行。
Do not stand at the door.	不要在车门处停留。
The limit measures will be taken because of the large passenger flow during peak hours, please wait patiently.	由于高峰时段客流较大，车站将采取限流措施，请您耐心等待。
Attention: this station is out of service because of emergency, please get off the station as quickly as possible and take other transportation. We apologize for any inconvenience this might cause.	乘客请注意：本站因故紧急关闭，请尽快有序出站，选择其他交通工具，不便之处，敬请谅解。
Please stand on the right and hold the handrail when you take the escalator.	请您在乘坐电梯时，紧握扶手，靠右站立。
Please cooperate with the security check, get off first and do not crowd.	主动配合过安检，先下后上勿拥挤。
This train is going back to the station, please don't get on the train and wait for the next one, thank you for your cooperation.	本次列车为回库列车，在本站清车不上人，请等候下次列车，感谢您的配合。
We are sorry to inform that the train is out of service, please get off the train and take other transportation. We apologize for any inconvenience this might cause.	由于列车故障，请有序下车或选择其他交通工具。对此带来的不便，敬请谅解。
The last train to the … station is gone, please take other transportation, thank you.	开往某方向的末班车已发出，去往某站的乘客请您换乘其他交通工具。
Attention: please do not crowd in rush hours, the next train is coming, please wait for the next train patiently.	乘客请注意：由于现在候车乘客较多，请您分散候车，上不去车的乘客请您等候下次列车。
Attention: the train is out of service for emergency, please get off the train as quickly as possible. You can wait for the next train or take other transportation. We apologize for any inconvenience this might cause.	乘客请注意：列车因故无法继续载客运行，请您尽快离开车厢，在站台等候下次列车或选择其他交通工具。不便之处，敬请谅解。

附录3
文明用语

英文	中文
Please follow the rules to keep the order well.	为了保障良好的乘车秩序，请您自觉遵守地铁的各项规定。
May I help you?	您好有什么需要帮助的吗？
Please queue up for tickets.	请排队购票。
Please keep quiet.	请保持安静。
Excuse me, please wait a moment. I will ask other staff for help.	不好意思，请稍后，我将问询其他工作人员。
Which station do you want to go? It is ...yuan.	请问您想去哪站，票价为……
How much would you like to recharge?	请问您想充值多少钱？
Please do not litter.	请勿乱丢垃圾。
Please hold the handrail for your safety.	为了您的安全，请握住扶手。
The door is going to close, please wait for the next train.	车门即将关闭，请等待下一班列车。
Take it easy, I will try my best to help you.	别着急，我会尽量帮助您。
Please follow the instructions of the staff, thank you.	请您配合工作人员的指挥，谢谢。
Please use headphones to listen to music or watching videos.	听音乐或观看视频时请使用耳机。
Please offer your seat to those in need.	请为需要的人士让座。
Have a nice trip, goodbye.	祝你旅途愉快，再见。

附录4 劝阻用语

英文	中文
The train to …station is coming, please keep clear of the screen door.	开往某方向的列车即将进站，请您不要倚靠屏蔽门。
Attention please: for everyone's safety, no smoking in the station. Please have the security check, dangerous goods are not allowed in the train.	乘客请注意:为了您和他人的候车安全，严禁在站内吸烟。请自觉接受安检，严禁携带易燃易爆等危险品进站乘车。
Do not push or shove when boarding.	上车时请不要推挤。
Don't hand out advertisements in the train or station, no begging or performing.	请勿在车站及车厢内派发广告，乞讨卖艺等行为。
Don't chase, fight or go skateboard, roller skating, bike-riding or other sports.	请勿在车站、车厢内追逐、打闹或从事滑板、轮滑、自行车等运动。
Please do not use your phone in a loud manner.	请不要大声使用你的手机。
Don't walk in the wrong direction when you take the escalator.	请勿在运行的自动扶梯上逆行。
No smoking in the subway.	地铁内禁止吸烟。
Don't use the security equipment in non-emergency situations.	请勿在非紧急状态下动用紧急或安全装置。
Mind the gap between the train and the platform.	注意列车与站台之间的空隙。
Don't stay at the entrance, exit and gate entrance.	请勿在车站出入口、疏散通道内、闸机口处滞留。
Don't get on and off the train forcibly.	请勿强行上下车。
Don't climb or step over the fence net.	请勿攀爬、跨越护栏护网。
Don't get into the gate without permission.	请勿违规进出闸机。